The Last of England

by the same author

poetry
FOX ON A BARN DOOR
THE SOLITARIES
THE NIGHT BATHERS
GLOVES TO THE HANGMAN
BURNING THE IVY
HANDS AT A LIVE FIRE: SELECTED POEMS

stories
YOU'VE NEVER HEARD ME SING

autobiography
THE HIGH PATH

travel
IN SPAIN

The Last of England
TED WALKER

JONATHAN CAPE

LONDON

First published 1992
©Ted Walker 1992
Jonathan Cape, 20 Vauxhall Bridge Road, London SW1V 2SA

Ted Walker has asserted his right
under the Copyright, Designs and Patents Act, 1988
to be identified as the author of this work

Excerpt from 'Everyone Sang' by Siegfried Sassoon
reproduced by permission of George Sassoon, Note from the
Collected Poems by Dylan Thomas reproduced by permission
of David Higham Associates, 'Halnaker Mill' by Hilaire Belloc
from The Complete Verse of Hilaire Belloc reproduced with
permission of the Peters, Fraser & Dunlop Group Ltd

A CIP catalogue record for this book
is available from the British Library

ISBN 0-224-03211-9

Phototypeset by Computape (Pickering) Ltd, North Yorkshire
Printed in Great Britain by
Mackays of Chatham PLC, Chatham, Kent

For
The Grandchildren
With
The Love
That Will Survive
Of Us

I've changed some names of course

ONE

HE HAD a digging fork across his back, slung with hefty cord; he strode out ramrod straight, as an infantryman beginning a route march; and he was pushing a home-made wooden barrow full of gardening tools. On the phone in the living-room, I watched him turn down Church Lane and disappear from view. I hung up peremptorily, slammed out of the house and chased after him. He was half-way down the lane by the time I caught up. The tines of his fork were safely embedded in a wooden guard; so, long ago, had I used to carry my fork, when I went to dig for lug-worm at low tide. I walked just behind him for a little way, wondering what words to use and what manner to adopt: despite an educated accent and middle-class clothes, I was still, at fifty-two, the son of my carpenter father, awkward in the role of prospective employer. We had almost reached the small dell of hedgerow trees, where a mud path strikes off from the lane and leads to the allotments. The tools clinked and chinked in the barrow, and I could see their clean steel in the Maytime sun, their handles and shafts as shining and smoothened with long use and wear as the sprung maple dance-floors of my youth. There was a galvanised watering can in the barrow too, endearingly dented and with a brass rose; and lengths of sisal, and bamboo canes, and some slatted seed boxes, and a dibber made from an old spade handle; also a trug on a hessian sack that probably smelled of creosote. No polythene, no plastic, no nylon. The year was 1987, but he was exactly as retired working men had looked when I was a small boy during the War. In just such a cloth cap, just such sturdy boots, colourless flannels and jacket, his like would forever be coming and going between home and the allotment plots: Digging For Victory, bringing home a bucket of spuds or a feed of beans. He'd have been pushing a cart just like this one; or, laboriously, his Wellington-booted toes outward-pointing, he'd have been pushing the pedals of an upright and elderly Hercules bike; and there'd have been a cabbage-box tied to the handlebars, in which would ride a terrier worn out from ratting. Everything about this old fellow I was following seemed to betoken a version of England I had somehow mislaid or disremembered.

'Excuse me,' I said, out of breath, overweight, ridiculous beside his leanness. 'I hope you won't think me rude, but I just wondered if you'd be interested in taking on some part-time work?'

He stopped and, still gripping the barrow handles, took his time to size me up. His eyes were rheumy, pale blue behind their glistening and the round lenses of his mended specs. On the backs of his hands were melanoma scabs and the spreading sepia mottlings of old age. I didn't expect a straight or immediate answer. In Sussex, old people give out information and opinions in cautious syllables; non-committal, grudging, dribbled like a tight pinch of expensive seeds: enquiries after someone's obviously blooming good health will prompt the dispiriting response, 'fair to middling'; and, of even the most saintly soul, it will never be allowed more than 'he has his good faults.'

'Couldn't rightly say,' he began. But he set down the barrow, indicating that our parley might continue. 'What with one thing and another.' He was nervous, gentle, a man who perhaps had not always been as mild as he now appeared. It was as though his voice had recently had an old strength knocked out of it.

'It's like this,' I said. 'My wife has just died – '

'Oh dear.'

' – and I'm going away for a little while, and I need

somebody to look after the garden.'

'Well, I don't know ...'

'Just a few hours a week.'

'I've got ten rods of allotment of my own, look. As well as keeping an eye on somebody else's while they're laid up. Garden at home into the bargain.'

I knew where he lived, for now I recognised him as the man I'd seen stooping at work in front of his bungalow along the Barnham Road. He had a shrub of southernwood growing beside the pavement – the plant also known as Old Man, or Lad's-Love. I'd once had a fine specimen growing outside my back door, but it had long since died; every year, when I taught Edward Thomas's poem 'Old Man' to a class in my college, it was from this old man's Old Man that I filched a small fistful of the 'hoar-green, feathery herb' so that the students could shrivel the tips and smell its bitter scent. I had been a common thief, thieving late at night.

'Just keeping up with the weeds,' I said. 'And the grass to cut. There's a good motor-mower. There'd be no heavy digging.'

'Got a year or two left in me, maybe.' It was a reproach.

'Oh, a lot more than that, I'd say!'

'Rising eighty.'

'And there's my wife's grave. I'd need that looking after. I've got four children, but they all live too far away.'

'I could talk it over, with mercy.'

'I'm sorry?'

'That's Mrs Talbot. My wife, Mercy. I'm Jack.'

'It's a nice old garden, Mr Talbot. Ten-foot wall all round. Brick and flint. Mine's the white house opposite the Elm Tree Stores. There'd be nobody ever to bother you.'

It was this consideration that clinched it. As we talked, I learned that of recent times he'd found it harder and harder to share the company of others. Three hours a week, say, in my enclosed garden would suit him well. The money I was offering was much too much, he said; he didn't need money at his time of life, wouldn't know what to do with it. But we

3

agreed that he would find an envelope every Monday morning on a certain shelf in the shed, left there by my neighbour whom he would never see. So I said I'd see him next – well, I didn't know when. And he nodded, putting the garage key in a pocket that rustled as though with onion skins, and I went back home.

Not that it felt anything like a home any more. Lorna was five weeks dead. I had fallen in love with her when I was fourteen, and I had never been in love with anybody else. After the funeral my children had resumed their lives elsewhere. I had given away my cat. What I had now was a house too absurdly spacious for me, a premises. It enclosed its irrelevant furniture, its wardrobes and drawers containing clothes and miscellanea whose former owner no longer needed them and yet which I could not bring myself to part with or dispose of. They variously rebuked or mocked me. Blouses, collections of porcelain thimbles, half-finished knitting. I could have been no more lonely in a chaos of rocks.

I went out into the garden. I had told Jack Talbot it was nice: but I had lied, for now it was hateful to me; and this not only because it had become neglected. Twenty years before, when I was in my early thirties, I had bought the place from a strange, Anglo-Indian doctor called Campbell-Petters. The garden had been neglected then, because for a few years he had been renting it out to a series of feckless tenants. He still had his practice in the single-storey annexe: but when he had lived in the house he had kept the third of an acre in good heart, hugely abundant. Doctoring had been, indeed, something of a second string for him. The walled plot was his almost self-sufficient small-holding. His way of life, since the Thirties, had been that of many another rural G.P. In the ramshackle, lean-to green-house he had raised large, luscious, white-fleshed peaches, the surfeit of which were sent to Covent Garden. They'd fetched five shillings each, and the best of them (he assured me) had found their way to the Queen Mother's table. In an outhouse he had raised turkeys. He had had bee-hives. He had grown strawberries and raspberries, currants and gooseberries. The

4

June evening when I first took Lorna and the children to view the property, I followed the doctor this way and that through rampant nettles and ground elder, among the remnants of his former domain. Almost entirely curtained by the delicate, weeping fronds of a willow tree there was an ornamental pond, with water up to five feet deep, in which he had raised trout. There were two Bramley apple trees, a Laxton and a Cox's, and a greengage and a Victoria plum. Against the warm-facing walls there were spread-eagled a Conference pear and a Williams pear. And still there was room, in beds along the borders and simple geometries cut from the lawn, for flowering trees and shrubs – a magnolia, a purple buddleia – and a pergola of old-fashioned climbing roses, and rambling roses – Gloire de Dijon and Albertine; and standard roses, bush roses, and a moss rose exquisitely formed and scented and all but concealed in rampant overgrowths of periwinkle.

'If you buy the house from me,' the doctor said, 'you must promise me one thing. You see that small window in the outhouse? Every year, about the middle of April, you must leave it open so that the swallows can come and go.' I stood with the doctor for several minutes, while my children were in the house with their mother, bagging this room or that for themselves and making the dog bark and yap with the excitement and terror of coming to somewhere new, while the swallows came and went through the little window. I was happier, during those minutes, than I had ever been. We were all well, thriving, and I was moderately prosperous.

Now, twenty years on, and with every last pair of swallows having long since deserted, I stood in the self-same spot, knowing myself as unhappy as I had ever been. I had to get away, possibly for ever.

Indeed, possibly for ever and ever. I packed my little hatchback Fiat, not only with clothes and books and writing materials but also with a sizeable plastic box containing Lorna's left-over store of pain-killing drugs: morphine-based tablets, mainly, but also dozens of sachets of analgesic powder (known as *fizz-bangs* in the terrifying, arch jocularity of nurses) which, sprinkled on to a tumbler of water, would form a pale pink scum at the surface like that on a strawberry milk shake. Though I was not entirely unhinged at the time, I was certainly close to desperation: I could quite easily imagine myself preparing for a permanent exit somewhere in a quiet room, with an elaborate cocktail of tablets and brandy and pink fizz. For the moment, however, my compulsion was to escape from the well-meant – but ultimately agonising – kindness and pity of family, friends, colleagues and neighbours. For weeks now I had been eating their dinners, listening to their comfortable words on the telephone, reading their soft messages in letters, inviting them over my threshold when the doorbell rang; and they were not to know how incalculably worse was the ensuing aloneness when one had taken one's leave after the pudding, hung up the receiver, screwed up the envelope, dropped the Yale latch and returned to the furniture. Only the company of total strangers is acceptable during those astonished, early days of bereavement, when the semi-realisation is still not yet even half-accepted that the absence of the loved one is to be permanent; when it is still one's habit to call up the staircase with a question, to continue to lay out the other plate, to exclaim aloud at the sight of a robin on the bird-table, so that the pleasure in it may be shared.

I was on the point of leaving when I answered the door to a stout lady of a certain age. She was holding a half-bottle of gin as though it were a posy of flowers. 'I've brought this for you,' she said. 'Do you remember me? May I come in?'

A quarter of a century before, she had been a colleague of mine, very briefly, at an awful school in Bognor Regis. Then she had been a fat, young, jolly woman with fairly close-set eyes behind round-rimmed glasses; now she was a fat, middle-aged, grimmish woman with eyes that had moved immediately adjacent to the bridge of her nose. She had recently been widowed, she told me. She made an inspection of the house, upstairs and down. 'The entrance hall and the lounge would make a lovely *through-room*,' she said.

★

I was, so to speak, at the side of my own life: almost someone else, who watched what I did. Without my wife to be with and to care for, I was not what I had for so long been seen to be by the world. Nor was it solely (though it was overwhelmingly) a matter of having recently become a widower: for I felt I was no longer needed as a father (though I could expect to grow into a new familial role now that my grandson Jonathan had been born). Professionally, I walked in an empty cul-de-sac: my gift for poetry had long since deserted me, along with the treacherous swallows − and by now I was beginning to accept that it would never come back; and though my college had very kindly granted me compassionate leave of absence with pay, I did not have it in mind ever to return to the classroom: because I was drained, and because I felt that what I had once had to give was no longer wanted by the kind of students I would have to teach. My creative energy had dried, and I was physically debilitated by weeks and months and years of looking after my poor, broken-bodied wife. So I was no longer truly myself but rather someone masquerading within my ludicrous husk. It seemed plainly a nonsense, the business of prolonging the task of being, now that I was in the guise of a sham self, one deprived of his essential former functions. It's not that I felt particularly sorry for myself − though I had always been capable of self-pity; rather, I had an unaccustomed taste of bitterness on my lips and the smell of cynicism in my nostrils. I had found a propensity to sneer and to belittle those around me: not from a sense of superiority, I think, but from a deep-seated, if unacknowledged, need to distance myself. When I laughed it was with an emotion a long way removed from fun, and when I had to converse and commune with others, it was not with the spontaneity of natural good will but the sinister calculation of charm. I did not much care for myself.

I drove off the ferry at Dieppe, and had to wait a long time in the Customs queue while the van in front of me, packed tight with building materials, was methodically and sadistically ransacked by officials. I sat in the late afternoon sunshine, almost pleasurably, while many lengths of copper pipe were off-loaded, held up to the light and squinnied through as though they were components of optical instruments – in a fruitless search for, I supposed, illicit drugs. Had the *douaniers* chosen to take out their frustrations on me, and discovered my cache of proscribed narcotics, I suppose I might have been in serious trouble. My turn came; I handed my passport and car documentation through the window, and was ordered to get out and open the hatch door.

'How long do you intend to remain in France?'

'Three or four days. I'm on my way to Spain.'

'What is the purpose of your visit?'

There was little purpose in anything I did, but I could hardly tell the man that.

'Recuperation,' I said. 'My wife has just died. I've been lent an apartment on the Costa del Sol and –'

'You need not tell me the story of your life, *monsieur*. Get back in your car.'

I did as he said. The unfeeling bastard, I thought, may he rot for ever in hell. What did he know or care about anything that really mattered in life? He handed back my papers, put his face close to mine and said quietly, 'I am very sorry for you. I, too, have recently lost my wife. A cancer, you understand?'

'Same here.' I tried to frame a sentence expressing sympathy, but he slapped the roof. I moved forward and saw in the mirror how he was already beginning to give the driver behind me a hard time.

Using no maps, navigating only by the position of the sun and choosing minor roads, I was soon away from the raft of British cars and caravans which had disembarked with me. I stopped often, at cross-roads bars in villages or in the *grand'place* of some small market town, not because I needed coffee or a beer but because I needed to practise my adopted identity. My French was still fluent.

The dimension of a different language is liberating; you find things to say in it that you do not feel the need to say in your own, and in a manner that releases unexpected slants on your opinions and surprising nuances in the manner of your saying them. I had no travelling companion. Nobody knew who I was or what my troubles were. I was not subject to the tyranny of time – whether measured by the clock or the calendar – and nobody who was related to me or was otherwise of my acquaintance knew my whereabouts.

And quite abruptly, along a straight stretch of unspoilt arable country, I felt a sense of freedom, blithe. It was good to be abroad. I willed myself to be, in a sense, stateless. There was a General Election brewing, and I was thankful to be having no part of it. Twice before, in 1979 and 1983, I had left Britain for three-month spells of working in Spain while a General Election was taking place. It looked certain that Mrs Thatcher would win a third term. The prospect sickened me. I realised how much I had come to despise the England that England had become; the new, awful sort of Englishness of the English, the squalor, the hard-nosed self-seeking, the philistinism, the heart-lessness, the yobbish bad manners of so many ordinary people, the hypocrisy and ruthless contempt of the current ruling class for the true old-fashioned qualities of life and the living of it by such as Jack Talbot. I pulled over on to the grass verge and turned off the engine and listened to the birdsong and gazed at the spring flowers under the hedgerow; and was overcome with a ten-minute spell of convulsive and uncontrollable weeping: not from the grief that held my being in suspension – I had not yet properly begun to shed those tears – but from the realisation that, if I so chose, I should never again have to live in my home, or my homeland, now that they were spoiled beyond possible redemption.

Sudden outbursts of crying or laughter punctuated my gentle progress southwards. I would be moved to tears by the simplest, most commonplace beauty: the colour of a cow's tongue, the long spittle viscously trailing from it and catching the sun; a little girl with her mother by a fountain, happily exclaiming at the rainbow held in the cascading drops, and she not knowing yet what suffering was; an avenue of pleached lime trees announcing a village, branch ends resting on each other's shoulders like a line of Greek dancers. I must often have made a spectacle of myself, boo-hooing in public places, unable to prevent and then to staunch my weeping. And it was the same with laughter. The world could change in an instant from being ineffably lovely and sad, into its other, rude clown's outfit; when all seemed farcical, mad, irrational, informed by the Almighty's infinite mockery of His creatures. In a *pâtisserie* window I saw an ordinary confection − not unlike an Eccles cake − got up into a Byzantine presentation of different-coloured ribbons and bows, all set inside a kind of wicker-work cornucopia. It was an extreme example of excessively camp style − all form and minimal content − ubiquitously found in France. In no way funny − in fact it was enough, with its jejune frills and nauseating hues, to dispirit a sensitive soul − it ignited my shortest of emotional fuses, and I saw in the wretched concoction a very metaphor of the vanity of human endeavour; and coming to me so soon after a daily experience of the plain wrappings of wounds and the undisguisable facts of illness, pain and death, the droll cosmetics of the pastrycook's art had me giggling, though not with gaiety, fit to bust.

The first few nights I put up in the kind of shabby, fadedly genteel hotel where an iron and brass key (large enough to shift the wards of a castle lock) admits one to a room mustily odorous; with rose-patterned, ineptly hung wallpaper, wood-work varnished and grained, and with a view beyond net curtains and louvred shutters on to a market square ever full of revving two-stroke motorbikes after dark. I have no romantic or nostalgic affection for such establishments: for an overnight stay, I would much prefer somewhere mould-free, if ugly, with an *en suite* American bathroom, and a pillow that is not one of those intractable cylinders rolled into the end of the sheet. But I was tired out, and it could be said that the peeling, one-star Lion d'Or, the creaking Hôtel du Centre, the ruinous Hostellerie de l'Avenir, still perform a useful function, being the apt, temporary repositories of the melancholy of transient visitors. The sound of crying in them is not, one feels, a novelty; that bent-cane chair is no longer astounded by sobs, and involuntary snivellings seem well in tune with the long, dry sighings of superannuated plumbing. The wardrobe with the jamming door and the camphor smells left behind by clothes of the long-since dead seem to coagulate in their droplets on to one's stowed litre of whisky. There is always a church clock hard by to wake the sleeper with its cracked chimes upon every quarter hour, once the two-strokes have finally ceased their racket and until the hour of the pre-dawn, when the nearby bantam roosters crow. In such hotels I ate curious dinners (one was of some stuffed fowl gizzards) and got methodically drunk; then drank some more, and in my stupefaction lay in a stripey half-light, incapable of movement, feeling terminally ill.

Three nights of this were enough, however. I had brought camping gear, and when I reached Rochouart I pitched my tent on a sloping campsite not yet officially open for the season, and persuaded myself that the smell of canvas and the feel of cold on the cheek were good for me. Not that they were. I had no light to read by after a cheerless dinner of pilchards and inadequately ripened Camembert. I heaved my bulk over and over, like a beached whale, listened to the soundings of owls and the inconsolable howlings of dogs, and I myself added to the place's essential eeriness by singing along quietly with my radio until my second bottle of burgundy was emptied to the last slops. I spent one further night in France – in the cacophonous, egregious, lout-thronged centre of Tarbes – then climbed at mid-morning to the centre of the Pyrenees.

Another language, another identity, another personality. The Spanish frontier post was in a swirl of low cloud and trimmed with frost. The two Customs men were jolly, talkative, welcoming.

'How long do you propose to stay in Spain?'

'Possibly for ever. It's like coming home.'

'You are allowed ninety days.'

'In that case, eighty-nine days. Then I'll cross into Portugal for a night, and come straight back. Maybe I'll die here – who knows?'

They thought that this was wonderfully amusing: Spaniards quite enjoy larking about with the topic of death. I fetched the last of my whisky into their quarters for the three of us to have a tot before I began the long series of hairpins down from the pass. Even that high up, in the pure winds and the freshening spring leafage and pockets of old season's snow, you begin to detect the essential smells of rustic Spain. And the moment you approach even the smallest habitation, your nostrils are tickled by an unforgettable, antediluvian odour: one compounded of God knows what alchemy of cheeses racked in barns, the lees of local wines tainted with oak, the squirtings of nocturnal animal musks, matted hay in lean-to outhouses, high-stacked pine logs oozing resin; also pickled comestibles not known to northern Europe, steeped in herby olive oil. In a constricted passage of the road a herd of goats confronted me. I stopped, and became a midstream boulder against their current; they spilled alongside the car, some brushing it, until the goatherd chivvied the final stragglers past and gave me a nod. In my rear-view mirror they became remnants of the clouds I had left behind.

Loneliness and solitude, solitariness and aloneness; exile, apartness, isolation, separateness and seclusion: all of these are distinct. Some are states which are absolutely desirable from time to time – particularly for the artist – and which I had often chosen and actively sought out, ever since childhood. But some of them, if they have not been willingly pursued and embraced, soon erode the morale and sap the spirit. They bear down thick and stifling, noxious as industrial smog, and within a very short while even the most sociable and extroverted person can find himself gradually edged towards the reclusive habit. Of my own volition I had left home, alone, at a time when (customary wisdom would have you believe) one should welcome the presence and availability of friends and neighbours, family and colleagues: so serve me right, I thought, as I drove hour by hour through the barren uplands of Castile and Aragon, if I sometimes felt like howling into canyons just for the sound of my own echo. But I had chosen to do what I had done precisely because I had found the grief-pangs to be made worse by sympathisers: at best they offered platitudinous wishes and thoughts, which it sapped my energy to accept with a show of sincerity; and at worst they made impertinent intrusions, with all their proferred advice and pot-plants. It was, no doubt, all well-meant and kindly, but it was all equally useless. At that blackest of times there was no consolation. I had been severed from the one person whose love I wanted, and none of my store of love for her could reach her now. It could not be redirected towards our two sons and two daughters – split up fairly several ways between her legatees, like five-pound notes or bric-à-brac. I could not, and would not, give of myself to anyone any more; and the corollary was that I could no longer accept from, or share with, others whom it was my duty – and my now suppressed desire – to love and care for. It shames me to think that I scarcely considered, at that time, how my children might have been affected by their mother's death. Perhaps one of the most pernicious symptoms of my bereavement was that it temporarily impaired my capacity for displays of familial affection. It was as though something had lodged immovable within me, which brewed, festered, poisoned, and made all rancid.

Having shunned friends, and finding the occasional company of strangers only briefly palliative – like half an aspirin taken during a chronic tooth-ache – I decided it was time to look up old acquaintances. I had dozens of them, perhaps hundreds, scattered through every province of the country. Most of them had been struck up several years before, while I was researching my travel book, *In Spain*. But it was towards Cuenca I began to accelerate: in Cuenca, several summers before, I had lived alone for three months, without a car, living in a cheap small hotel and writing a book of autobiography called *The High Path*.

It is axiomatic that one should Never Go Back. The cheap hotel which had been my home for twenty pounds a week had clad itself in hideous, shiny, reconstituted marble of a colour unknown to geology. Its pretensions and rates had quadrupled. The three down-at-heel, slightly *louche* but ever warm-hearted and chatty old fellows who had shared shift duties on the reception desk had been replaced by brisk youngsters whose anonymous, American-style efficiency, newly laundered shirts and professional courtesy seemed to rebuff any possibility of even the smallest of small talk.

While checking in I tried to make some, none the less. In my best Castilian, I commented on the immediately apparent changes. I said how I'd lived there for three months once, how fond I'd been of the place, and so on, but I trailed off in mid-sentence, for I realised I was being a garrulous bore in the way people are when they've had nobody to talk to for some time: a new bad habit to guard against.

The young man handed me my key. He spoke in English, with a disc-jockey accent I suppose he had picked up in a language lab.

'You will be impressed by the wonderful ameliorations, sir,' he said.

My pleasant little box, with its roll-down, green slatted blind and tesselated balcony, had been subsumed (by some baffling interior remodelling) into a duplex of double rooms on floors which seemed to be at different levels from the ones I remembered. I took one at approximately the height memory demanded, broke a fingernail tugging open the double glazing and stared down at a street now without its traffic policeman and horribly dragooned by parking meters. The balconies opposite still had their linear aviaries of singing birds, however, and the great, overloaded timber trucks still lurched and ground their gears and hissed their airbrakes at the red lights stopping their progress towards the sawmills.

The trilling of canaries reminded me of how I had felt when I had first installed myself in the hotel, exactly eight years ago to the day.

That period, too, had been a watershed in my life. The year before, I had been awarded the Society of Authors' Travel Bursary. It had been my romantic intention to march from the Bay of Biscay to the Mediterranean, back-packing, sleeping under the stars, writing poems and stories in the shade of trees during the *siesta* hours and living on bread, sausage, fruit and wine. I had broken in new hiking boots, acquired one of those light-weight rucksacks and a light-weight tent and sleeping-bag to carry in it. My life had become a messy jumble that needed a good tidying; getting away for a spell would be good not only for me but for all those round me.

But one morning Lorna had woken to find a little stain of blood on her pillow. It happened the next day, too, and the next. After about a week, I noticed how she would occasionally put a handkerchief to her face, as though she had a sniffly cold.

It became clear that these had been no ordinary nose-bleeds: there had been too little blood for them to have been that. Neither of us could have forecast that a spot of blood on a white pillow was – as Keats had described such a discovery once in Rome – a death warrant.

An E.N.T. consultant confidently stated that the tumour on the bone of the nose had almost certainly been caught in time. Lorna had her operation on about the date when I would have been setting off for Spain – she had even tried to insist that I should not change my plans for what she maintained was only a minor inconvenience – and through that summer I nursed her, then took her twice a week for radiotherapy to a hospital in Portsmouth; and the following spring she seemed to be as right as ninepence, with nothing more to show for the experience than an all but indetectable, inch-long curving scar along the crease between her nose and her right cheek.

By the time the following May was approaching, I had changed my idea about the nature of my intended sojourn in Spain: romanticism gave way to pragmatism; a quiet but persistent inner voice told me I ought to be continuously reachable from home, not incommunicado in the tractless sierras; so, instead of tramping across the country from sea to sea like some latter-day Laurie Lee, I would select one place and stay there.

When the end of the academic year approached (I worked for the British campus of an American college whose second semester finished at the end of the first week in May) at lunch-times I walked the quiet lanes nearby and watched spring approach with my release. I saw the celandines come into bloom, and the cuckoo-flowers and primroses, and crossed my fingers in the earnest hope that nothing would stop me from getting away. Though Lorna appeared to be fit and well, her parents (whom we had taken in to live in our annexe) sometimes gave us concern. Her mother, strenuously anti-life, a perpetual moaner and moral blackmailer, might very well have willed herself to produce symptoms of any alarming disease she chose, up to the very eve of my departure. I was to be consumed with such unworthy but entirely justifiable thoughts as these until the ferry cast off at Plymouth: I knew her sly, thwarting methods of old.

What I felt in Cuenca now was a mixture of grief, ghastly emptiness and the beginnings of remorse; what I had felt in Cuenca on my previous arrival had been a mixture of guilt, elation, and the dread of possible imminent artistic failure.

I had long since discovered the truth, confirmed by Cyril Connolly's *Enemies of Promise*, that domesticity gets in the way of a writer's progress. Well, I had chosen to be a family man before I had begun to publish, and if I had had my time over again I would not have done otherwise: but the urgency to get cracking on a twenty years' backlog of unwritten words was uncomfortably pressing. At my age, I should have accomplished far more than I had.

The guilt I toted to Spain in 1979, however, was not easily put aside before I could begin. Not guilt on account of having appropriated any family money for my jaunt: anyway, though we had little to spare, we weren't absolutely hard up; it wasn't as though we were living on turnip soup or dressing ourselves in jumble-sale clothes. And it was not that I'd be giving up a good job in some vague though earnest hope of holing up to write a bestseller: the salary for my college teaching post would continue to be paid through the long summer vacation, and my travel and subsistence expenses were all to come from the £750 bursary. No. The problem lay in absenting myself at all, let alone for three months. For how *could* I go swanning off abroad for such a length of time, leaving my wife to cope with my responsibilities as well as her own? Chaps like me didn't do things like that, did they?

There had been, of course, plenty of proletarian writers – poets, novelists, playwrights – establishing themselves since the end of World War II, but they were still a frankly newish phenomenon, uncomfortable and clumsy in the gentleman's world of publishing and the exotic gentilities of the literary Establishment: persons without inherited money to allow them to see the world beyond their own doorsteps, but also having the cultural millstone of domesticity round their necks. Once you were married – and certainly once you had children – you were in honour bound to acquire and to stick to a safe, no matter if tedious, job until retirement. If you wrote, or painted, or whatever, this was assumed to be a hobby not unlike constructing models out of matchsticks. Whether or not it was in haste that you married, if you were an artist you repented at long leisure from wedding to funeral. If you harboured occasional thoughts of swaggering the nut-strewn roads, and if you voiced those thoughts, you were brusquely informed by a Voice of Conscience booming down the generations that 'You should have thought about that in the first place, my lad,' or (to preclude any further discussion) 'You'll do what you want, just like you always do.' Not that one often, if ever, did; for, if you did clear off, you got dubbed a right bastard to be shunned by family, relatives and friends as a moral pariah. Few writers of my acquaintance with origins similar to mine had satisfactorily resolved this essentially English, educated-working-class dilemma without distressing upheavals. Husbands had no business to go 'gallivanting off' unless they had the kind of job – soldiering, sailoring, long-distance lorry driving – that obliged them to. Hence, many poets of the Sixties were perforce of the 'Pram In The Hall' school, their subject matter sneered at by mandarin reviewers. Many fiction writers and dramatists were creating works which, though they may have had genius, were necessarily provincial, parochial or – the ultimate microcosm – 'kitchen sink'. Small worlds, from which their creators cannot escape, have often provided material for great literature, as Jane Austen's novels prove; and some writers – Larkin was a good example – have loathed the very idea of travel: but these instances are not sufficient to refute the argument that what a writer must have is independence of means and freedom of action. In 1929, Virginia Woolf had pleaded, on behalf of women writers, for a room of one's own and £500 a year, which was a lot of money then. All of half a century later, no one (as far as I knew) was pleading the cause of the working-class family-man writer. Small literary prizes, of which I had won several, were tokens of recognition and encouragement, but they bought little time and certainly offered no possibility of independence. Feminism, a cause I have always espoused, exacerbated certain injustices for men such as me: for surely one corollary of sexual freedom and equality should have been the removal of the oppressively heavy moral obligation on husbands and fathers to be the ultimately responsible bread winners and strong, protective, ever-present arms. Virginia Woolf had a good case – it's one that still hasn't been adequately answered – but I bet it was old Leonard who would have got summonsed if they hadn't paid the rates.

Could I go? Should I go? Would I go? The only condition imposed on me upon becoming the recipient of the Travel Bursary was – reasonably enough – that I should go abroad on the money.

However, for anyone born in my particular narrow band of the class spectrum – of an artisan, Puritan, Protestant Work Ethic, Band of Hope, Co-operative Wholesale Society, Left Book Club, Pledge-signing, Paying on the nail, Fabian, Complete Works of Dickens, Sunday School background – a husband leaving home to pursue his own selfish ends would have merited, not so long before, a concert of 'Rough Music' outside his front door: a cacophony of clashing pans and dustbin lids to accompany a banshee choir of local dis-approvers.

But I was going, and that was that.

A friend kindly offered to drive me to Reading station to catch a train for Plymouth. My leave-taking was portentous and full (I fancied) of implied censoriousness: none of it emanating from Lorna herself, though she was – as I was – understandably upset at the prospect of our longest absence from each other since her college days, years before our marriage. All the family, including Lorna's parents, lined up outside the house to wave me goodbye. They grouped themselves into a kind of tableau, like wedding guests for a photograph. We had eaten a roast lunch together, the children who had left home having made a special effort to come and see me off. My mother and father, too, were members of the valedictory party, a party rendered even more glum for me by sporadic outbursts of arch jocularity. I was wearing one of those light blue denim, Marks and Spencer 'safari' jackets with patch pockets, so handy for a traveller's documents and such; and had I been crowned with a solar topee and been carrying an elephant gun instead of a cardboard suitcase and a portable typewriter, the solemn extraction by my father of promises to keep in touch and injunctions by my mother to take great care of myself (I was forty-four years old) might have been more pertinent. It was as though I was thought secretly intent upon plunging into unknown, plague-ridden bush country or departing, under-equipped and *sans* string vests, on an unaccompanied expedition by Snocat to the South Pole. Lorna was shedding tears she had held back until now: I did not mind them, we had had ten minutes on our own and all was well between us. But her mother was beginning to comfort her – quite needlessly, and with a disingenuous theatricality, as though I was to be lost for ever; and she was no doubt already rehearsing another full-blown fit of her own perennial miseries. The car engine was running. 'Put your foot down, mate,' I muttered, smilingly waving and blowing kisses. And we moved off.

The countryside of the southern counties looked more golden and glorious than in any year I could remember: I had never seen so many closepacked and big-bloomed dandelions in the pastures. England was at her most delectable, fresh as a salad. It was warm – cuckoo and nightingale time – skies freshly rinsed and rose-buds in suburban gardens plumping up. 'I've got no business to be going off like this,' I said, more than once; and my friend offered to turn round and take me home there and then. He was a writer, too. I think it amused him – more professionally, maybe, than as a friend – to observe my moral wrestlings. His mischievous needling strengthened me.

'Poor Lorna,' he said. 'She'll be a grass widow.'

'Got to go. Might never have the chance again.'

'Cheer up, then!'

But Lorna would not, could not, have done as I was doing. Own up, I thought. It cut both ways: wives could not go swanning off, either. For the space of several miles, I visualised her indeed as a widow: me not being there with her, she weeding the garden and feeding the chickens and quite often doing nothing but cry. Not that I often had such morbid thoughts; but whenever I did, I always assumed I would be the first of us to die.

My elation upon taking possession of that little room in Cuenca was overwhelming; also, short-lived and unrepeatable as moments of euphoria usually are. I had experienced elation as often (or as seldom) as, I suppose, most people do: on first making love, on settling in the train compartment bound for our honeymoon, on beholding our first-born; also, less conventionally, on letting fly a record-breaking discus throw, playing and landing a glistening carp, seeing the dust-jacket of a first book of poems with my name on it. I had not experienced it lately, however; and, while I unpacked my case and heard those canaries singing, I thought rather sentimentally of Siegfried Sassoon's poem and was

> fill'd with such delight
> As prison'd birds must find in freedom
> Winging wildly across the white
> Orchards and dark-green fields; on; on; and out of sight.

20

And this was because, though I had for many years been singing contentedly enough in my cage of domesticity, the songs had not been as they might be, perhaps, if the cage door were unwontedly left open for me to fly free, if I chose to.

Could suddenly-loosed, long-captive birds still fly, like those that are used to the wild? Would those canaries opposite my balcony continue to sing their hearts out as full-throatedly if they had the run of all the sunflower plantations and vineyards of La Mancha? Probably not. Brute yearning, precisely that, probably, made them call through the sunlight to their unattainable fellow-creatures. My elation evaporated at the actual prospect of assembling paragraphs on to the blank sheets. What if, having come by all the most propitious conditions, I now found nothing to write? Or, having something to write, could not do so well enough? If I failed now, I would have failed for good and all.

That evening, I had gone out and had begun to make new friends.

Now I was back, I would have gone out in search of them: Pedro, the Master Blacksmith, Eduardo, the painter-poet, and Alejandro, the restaurateur who looked like Sergeant Bilko. But while I brushed up and shaved and assembled a cheerful face, I dropped my denture in the wash-basin and it broke in two. I had had a similar accident here in 1979, and the bizarre coincidence filled me with an extra, if petty, despair. I looked at myself in the mirror, a toothless Pagliacio, and tried to speak some coherent words. I could not. In the midst of life, we are in farce.

TWO

Y OU TURNED INLAND by the Mosque and the King of Saudi Arabia's palace and climbed the mountain's hairpin bends until you reached a tarmac street with lampposts that might have come from Reigate. It was not the country I knew. Despite the aloes and the lizards and the roadside pomegranate trees, the immediate hinterland of the Costa del Sol had long since become a colossal raft of *ad hoc* development garnished with flags of all nations. A golf course, preternaturally green, sprawled across acres of what had once been parched scrubland. There were apartment blocks and timeshare villas; polyglot hoardings; restaurants offering the *cuisines* of every European and Middle-Eastern nation; more banks than bars; clubs for crooks and the respectable aged; here a tennis school, there a Mercedes agency, everywhere cranes, maybe a residual ox-drawn plough, much concrete being painted white. It was the last of Spain.

The area I was to inhabit for the summer was high above these worst excesses of the coastal strip, half-way between Marbella and San Pedro de Alcántara. It was a half-finished estate which might one day become not a village but rather a tight enclave, predominantly for the British. There was a communal swimming-pool at its highest point; but no shop yet, no telephone except the one in the Sales Office, and no café: just a few dozen houses and flats in three-decker layers built into the steep slopes round a single street the shape of a 9, complete with suburban kerbstones and the Reigate lamps. Its name was Cerros del Lago, Lake Hills, the lake being a vast, man-made reservoir damming the waters of a river that sprang somewhere in the inaccessible heights of the Serranía de Ronda. From the pool, there was a splendid vista of the Rock of Gibraltar and, on the rare occasions when the sea-mist lifted, of the high ground behind the Moroccan shore. A few more kilometres up the deeply pot-holed road, you came to a village called Istán, a real place whose citizens still managed to maintain their community's Spanish identity and integrity despite the creeping encroachment of foreigners relentlessly up towards their lovely mountainside fastness. The road petered out at its centre; to go beyond, up into the high *sierra*, you would have needed a pack animal, a strong pair of legs and a marked sense of adventure.

When I arrived, it was mid-afternoon and overwhelmingly hot, but I unloaded the car at once, needing, superstitiously, to have all the possessions I'd brought from England around me in my new home. There were two flights of stone steps down to the door, which opened on to a balcony with black iron railings overhanging a precipitous slope. Unobserved (for my neighbours up and down the hill would have surely been asleep, or lazing up at the poolside) I made perhaps a dozen journeys to and fro. Then I locked myself in and drew the curtains and, without bothering to unpack or even to explore the apartment, stripped off and got under the single sheet on the bed.

I was as exhausted as I ever have been in my life; already more debilitated than I knew by the extended stress of Lorna's long illness, her suffering and her slow dying, and then of my grief, I now had the ordinary, physical tiredness of having driven the length of France and Spain. The final leg had been one of three hundred tough miles, begun in Albacete in the hour before dawn. At first, I was too tired to sleep; the sounds of the road were strident in my inner ear, and its images were insistent behind my lids: exhaust-belching Pegaso trucks; billion-acre olive groves, *triste*, grey-silver; the cock-pheasant copper of Andalusian earth; the threatening cliffs and gulches of rock endlessly to be plunged under and round and through. In

Albacete I had been saddened to learn that the dentist who had attended me on a previous occasion had not long since died. Also my old drinking chum there, Jesús, had recently seen the light and nowadays broadcast every day without fail on local radio about the evils of liquor. I hadn't been able to bring myself to look him up – it seemed to me that, for a man in my state, a bottle of brandy would prove a more steadfast and reliable chum than a solemn renegade. All was in flux in life. Nothing, and no one, could be depended upon to be unchanging. The creatures that had peopled your habituated life metamorphosed in ways too baffling to contemplate, let alone explain. The jolly drinker (for Jesús had been no alcoholic) became a kill-joy – and this, all of a sudden. And the one you had loved for as long as you remembered, who could always be counted on to love you back, had become unwontedly absent, and would remain absent, and that was that. I cried for a little while, but not as many tears as I had yet to shed, and finally I fell into a short, much-tormented sleep.

What woke me was not so much the terrifying image of my dream – a fetid pit of wallowing and threatening reptiles – as the repeated, urgent percussions their horny tails made as they lashed from side to side. It was as though their bodies were made not of tissue and blood and bone, but of rattling, man-made substances like bricks and mortar, glass and plastic; and when I opened my eyes, though the sight of the dragons and salamanders was expunged, their clatterings went on inexorably.

It was, of course, someone hammering flat-handed on the door.

I made an impromptu *dhoti* of the sheet, drew back the curtains and applied the key to the french window, clumsily, for I hadn't yet learned the knack of it, and there was time enough while I tried to persuade the wards of the lock to shift, for me to size up the person beyond the glass. She was forty-ish, blonde, a fading beauty, one whose once (I had no doubt) attractive face materialism and remorseless sunlight were transforming into a hard-bitten mask with sunken eyes the sunlight never reached, and which seemed to project a kind of generalised distaste. In casual clothes the colours of Neapolitan ice-cream, she was the sort I associated with television ads for carpet cleaners. I'd guessed who she was: Vicky Warboys, who lived next door but one and who kept an eye on the apartment for my brother's friend Sally.

A few days before leaving England I'd received a letter from Sally, enclosing the key; she'd written to Vicky, she said, announcing my arrival and saying I should arrange for my mail to be forwarded to the school in San Pedro where Vicky taught, the postal service to Cerros del Lago being notoriously unreliable.

'What do you think you're doing?' she snapped, the instant I had the door open. 'Who are you? How did you get in?'

I told her my name, and what arrangements had been made. Hadn't she received Sally's letter?

She grimaced, a pantomime of incredulity.

'You'd better come in,' I said. I led the way, clinging to my loin-cloth, a fat, surrealist Gandhi.

Alarmingly, she went into the bedroom instead of following me past my array of dumped clutter into the living-room. She pushed open the sliding door of the wardrobe, disclosing a long rack of androgynous summer garments like the ones she was wearing; I assumed they were Sally's.

'I'll get these moved.' And she grabbed at them, half a dozen hangers in each hand, and dropped them on to the bed.

'There's really no need,' I said. 'There's ample room for my stuff as well as Sally's.'

'These are my brother's things,' she said. 'He's been sleeping here while he's staying with us. He's had a breakdown.' She turned on me when I offered to help. 'I can manage perfectly well,' she said.

During the interval between her two journeys with armfuls of clothes, I hurriedly dressed for the sake of my dignity. 'I'm sorry to be the cause of so much bother,' I said, before her second departure. 'Perhaps I should have called on you before letting myself in − to let you know I'd arrived.'

25

'It's no bother,' she said, with the awesome, impassive smiling of the wholly exasperated.

'I don't mind at all if your brother stays here. There are two beds – as well as the sofa-bed in the other room.'

'I told you – my brother's had a breakdown.'

Slow on the uptake, I didn't realise until later that evening, when I took up some of her brother's personal items – his Walkman and cassettes, his alarm clock and such from the bedside table – that his breakdown was of the mental kind; I had been supposing that he'd suffered a broken half-shaft, or something akin, while motoring along from Malaga. I was introduced to him, Max, a diminutive, shiny-bald, flinching fellow with a pleasant demeanour. He was the editor of a prominent Marxist publication: a splendid journalist whose writings I have immensely enjoyed since in the pages of *The Times*. I repeated my invitation for him to stay put in Sally's apartment for the rest of his holiday, or recuperative break, or whatever. We had much in common, I said, both of us having inky fingers, both of us needing to restore ourselves. There was no need for either of us to get in the other's way.

'I can't,' Max said, with a nervous glance in the direction of his sister. 'Vicky says the girls will double up.'

The girls were Vicky's daughters; agreeable, quiet-mannered and courteous teenagers. They were going to double up in the sense of sharing a bedroom, not (as I, for one wild moment, thought) at the prospect of their uncle sleeping under the same roof as a bizarre interloper who draped himself in a sheet. We chatted amiably for a while, the sisters and their uncle Max and I. The younger girl was an ace swimmer; the older one was a scholar, a real flier who wanted to go to her uncle's old Cambridge college.

'I'm sure you're too good for Cambridge,' I said. 'Go somewhere more worthy of you.'

'Oh yes? And where did *you* go?' demanded her mother.

'Cambridge,' I said.

It had not escaped my notice that Vicky had removed her T-shirt and was now sitting topless on the settee. All summer long, whenever I saw her – except when in town or driving to or from school – she would be clad in nothing more than a bikini bottom and, possibly, flip-flops: while cleaning the car, while watering her patio garden, while engaging in conversation over the gate with the gnarled old odd-job man, Juan. Given the acrimonious nature of our recent introduction to each other, her semi-nudity, now, in her living-room, in the company of her daughters and her brother, seemed to me to smack less of brazenness than insolence. For all that, her effrontery filled the entire room, like cigarette smoke; and when required to speak to her, I had to contrive to direct my eyes towards an ornament behind her left ear. (A curious thing, now: I seem to conserve the memory of one of her breasts being furnished with two nipples, one aureole overlapping the other like plates on the shelf of a Welsh dresser. This surely could not have been the case? Perhaps the image has proceeded from a subsequent vivid – but emphatically non-erotic – dream; or perhaps my retina fixed, as I tried to avert my gaze, creating some Picasso-like distortion of her torso, a flickering, two-planes effect, just at the edge of vision.)

Her husband, Gavin, arrived. He was tall, athletic, one cast from the narrow-browed, literal-minded and crew-cut Adonis mould. I had known him by the dozen in my long ago school-teaching days: the handsome but past-it gym master who, in the summer term, would be glimpsed from the staff-room window doing laboured, shacking circuits of the running track, clad only in a kind of inadequate thong, keeping fit for the following season's rugby refereeing. Gavin was, indeed, a schoolmaster – at the same school as Vicky; but he taught not P.E. but Geography.

It was explained to him who I was and why Max's clothes, not to mention Max, had been brought back into the apartment. I made some jokey banter. Max and the older girl chuckled; the younger girl smiled rather shyly, not quite understanding what I was on about but prepared for the possibility, if not of humour such as her generation appreciated, then at any rate of the genuineness of my offer of *good* humour.

Gavin and Vicky were not much given to easy laughter, or open to my pathetic efforts at propitiatory charm. They went into the kitchen and conferred for a while; and during their absence, and after they returned, I continued to be apologetic for the fiasco which had occurred. Not that it had been my fault, of course: but in my volatile emotional state I was prepared to say a scene-averting sorry, the way some people do when their feet are agonisingly trodden upon in a crowded Tube. I needed not to be upset about anything else. Also, I needed to be a good neighbour, and I needed to receive my mail, which depended upon Vicky's willingness to act as my postman. So that, when the Warboys came back from the kitchen, smiling like scalpels, and invited me to visit their school and talk about poetry to their senior pupils, I was gratified and relieved to sense that all was well. It didn't occur to me – absurdly slow on the uptake as I was on this matter as I had been about Max's breakdown – that the Warboys needed to ingratiate themselves with me as much as I needed to with them: they'd been allowing Sally's apartment to be used without Sally's knowledge or permission.

★

Every day, I swam. Most of the time, I had the pool to myself. The water was silky, refreshing, constantly changed and purified yet not tasting of chemicals. A length was about 25 yards; I would do about a mile of slow, easeful breast-stroke, frequently resting, trying not to think of the horrors of the recent months and years. Two feet below the surface – at the deep end, where an inlet pipe pushed in freshly pumped water – there was a delectable bubbling, tumbling, whirling, jacuzzi effect which, while I hung crucified to the hand-rail, sensuously massaged my spine. Most mornings I would arrive while the skin of the water was still taut; and it was a special pleasure to enter gently, without making a ripple, without hurting the perfect surface. There would often be swallows dipping and sipping at a few drowned midges, occasionally dampening the rufous-red bibs at their throats before lifting and wheeling and darting down again, sometimes within a few inches of my head. I have never been fond of artificial bathing places, whether indoors or outdoors: having taught myself to swim in the sea, when I was a boy, I have usually found unliving water uncongenial; but the pool at Cerros del Lago was perfection of its kind, and I was grateful for it. There was lush grass nearby to lie on, and beautifully maintained beds of flowers: marguerites, begonias, lilies, hostas and vines; and, slightly overhanging the pool, a group of three graceful young palm trees with new fronds about to burst from their tight envelopes. All around the pool there was stone crazy-paving of many subtle gradations of the palest pastel colours – the sort you glimpse fleetingly when the light is caught in a film of oil ghosting over a puddle. A pair of elegant iron gates admitted one to this splendid artifact. Once within, you could feel, without undue pretension, intimations of Paradise. You were overlooked by nothing but the bare summit of a mountain. There was no sound but for birdsong and the weird, small music of insects and half-heard and unintelligible human voices and laughter carrying from some way off. You could smell wild herbs, borne up from the lower slopes not so much by a breeze as by warm air rising: lavender and rosemary, marjoram and thyme. Before the great heat of the afternoon, there was a warmth as comfortable as a wrapping of towels fresh from an airing cupboard. I would lie on the water or on the grass, looking upward. There was an eagle that visited occasionally, quartering the valley that held the reservoir; sometimes, when I stood on the retaining wall of one of the flower-beds to gaze towards Gibraltar, I would be on a level with him, or even above. And if the eagle was elsewhere, a buzzard or two would use the high spaces, effortlessly circling, their feathers (as I saw them through binoculars) dusty brown and fluffed up, less like plumage than untidy sphagnum moss.

I would think, I must remember to tell Lorna about this, the way I had always used to when I was away from her: in some beautiful or interesting place, temporarily absent on some job of work. The most cruel pain of all occurred at such moments, when I tried to face the still unacceptable fact that I could never tell her anything ever again. Not about anywhere. Not about anybody. Not on the phone, not on a postcard. Moreover, despite my talk above of intimations of Paradise, I did not really believe – except sentimentally, and seldom – that there was any such place. Lorna was not there, though she had had faith in its existence. Her remains were in the village churchyard, but she was nowhere, and could share nothing of what I was continuing to enjoy. But was enjoying incompletely: for the beauty all around me would seem, in the bitter minutes while I gathered up my things and walked back to the apartment, inapt, pointless, an irrelevance for a companionless Adam.

Within a few days, I became obsessional about housework. It was, I suppose, a kind of gesture of defiance, a gobbing in the face of my widowerhood. I had known men who, abruptly left alone – through divorce or bereavement – adopted a life of increasing squalor. They fed themselves with teaspoons straight from the unheated can; they refused to learn how to set the programme on a washing machine, or to acquaint themselves with the mysteries of the steam iron; the very whereabouts of Hoovers, brooms and mops in their homes remained arcane secrets from them. One fellow I had once talked to in my village pub, a decorated World War II fighter pilot, described to me how he sat every day among his soiled linen, old milk bottles and dust-furred knick-knacks and trophies, waiting for the postman to bring him news of an available room in the RAF Benevolent Home. Pathetic as this was, I think that for a while I became even more abject. I might easily have acquired an unbreakable new bad habit: of tidying up what was already in perfect order, of laundering what was pristine, of sweeping where there was no evidence of the slightest particle to chivvy with my broom. Before breakfast, I put my bedclothes out to air on the balcony. After washing-up, I made the bed and hung out my daily load of washing to dry on the line, with the pegs which I had specially acquired. I mopped the white tile floors until not one hair from my head could be found on them. I plumped cushions before they had had the chance to become unplumped. I cleaned all the windows, inside and out. Meticulous with my attention to the yokes, collars and cuffs of my shirts, I ironed them, suspended them on hangers from the curtain rail to sway until ready for folding and stowing away in their drawer. The instant I had drunk from a cup or eaten from a plate, I ran hot water and squirted green liquid. When there was nothing at all to do, I made infinitely small adjustments to the positions of books and paperclips; or used the loo or took a shower so that I could take a cleaning cloth once more to the porcelain or the screen. It would have been a short step for me from being a new widower to being a confirmed bachelor (or even an old maid) in my new, prissily fussing conduct in the home. I could have become like the mad, house-proud crone we once lived opposite, who, after the lightest shower of rain, would gather up the white flints from her rose-bed, carry them indoors in a pail, wash them under the kitchen tap, then replace them, innocent of the merest fleck of mud, precisely where they had lain before.

Emotional upheaval can easily upset one's entire psychological stability in ways like this. Personality and character may be changed out of all recognition during the temporary bafflement (but one does not know it is temporary) which must be survived and come to terms with. Imbalance appears permanent reality; what is eccentric, central. Just as I lost my sense of humour – and, therefore, my sense of proportion – when, as a fourteen-year-old, I first fell in love with Lorna, so I did now I was obliged to dismantle all but the memory of that love. A cloud of solemnity had enveloped several months of adolescence; in the new guise of suitor or swain (such as I knew from books) I became impervious to laughter, so seriously overwhelming was my amazing new state of being; and I must have cut as ludicrous a figure as it was possible to do, both with the adults who still would not admit me to their ranks and with my peers whom I affected to have deserted. And now, I was ludicrous again: the more so, because with maturity and long experience of life, I should have been able to stand outside myself and assess what was going on. How could I have let myself go down on my hands and knees to lift a fleck of dandruff from the floor with a moistened fingertip? Why did I drive to the Istán phone-box several evenings running and dial my home number, just to hear it ringing in an empty house?

There was something going on in my mind which I didn't understand: it was sinister and disturbing, whatever it was. I know this to be the case, on account of my behaviour during a short, sharp drama which occurred the last time I returned from my fool's errand to Istán.

There was just enough light shed by the streetlamp for me to see to the bottom of the two flights of steps. Beyond that, in the drop where a carob tree and a few scrubby herbs clung to precipitous rock outcrops and patches of soil almost too steep for human foothold, all was impenetrable darkness filling a small chasm packed with undergrowth, arbutus and pine. Beyond were the beginning slopes of the mountain, whose peak was barely discernible by fierce starlight. What made me hold my breath and take every step down with exaggerated caution was a single, dry rustling I heard from somewhere beyond where I could see – almost certainly from under the further arm of the L-shaped balcony projecting round two sides of the apartment.

I concluded at once that what I had heard was some nocturnal animal on the prowl. Perhaps it was only one of the mangy, skeletal cats that scratched a living round the edges of Cerros del Lago: but perhaps I might glimpse a fox, I thought; and I would have been grateful even for the snuffling companionship of a hedgehog. The area was still undeveloped enough to maintain an abundance of wildlife such as you might be lucky enough to see in all but wildest Spain. It would not have been too fanciful to hope to see a wild boar in those parts: I had already observed a pair of mongooses from the balcony, making short, scurrying dashes up and down the sheep runs, as well as snakes and lizards and all manner of shrews and voles. Once, while an invisible herd of goats was pursuing a tonk-

tonkling passage just beyond the mountain's foothill, I had seen a pack of feral dogs in a purposeful line making their way upwards. The naked eye had taken them for wolves; but the leading animals I saw through binoculars were scrawny, wolf-like Alsatians; and the dozen or so small followers and stragglers were a squalid, mixed bunch of mongrels. Thinking they might be rabid, I was as afraid for the goatherd as if they had, indeed, been wolves; and I decided always to keep a watchful eye open whenever I went on a scrabbling walk.

By now I had the knack of the awkward lock. As I turned the key, pressed down the handle and pushed the door stealthily back, I heard the rustling again. And then again, and yet again – more of a scraping this time than a rustle. And, as I was about to go inside and fetch the flashlamp out to circle the marauding little mammal in a pool of light, I heard, from only a few yards away in the pitch-black, first a cautionary hiss and then a muffled cough and agitated whisperings.

I was being burgled, by God!

I knew they were still outside. They were probably trying to force the little window just beyond where the balcony ended and where the ground reached just high enough up the wall to give access to the kitchen to a man on tiptoe or – more likely – standing on another man's shoulders. Blood rushed to my brain, as did Spanish vocabulary I didn't know I had. These were prompted perhaps by the anxious snatches I heard in the whispers – by now, frantic stage whispers – uttered in the thickened phonemes of *andaluz* dialect. I leaned over the railing and saw them. There were three: I could make this much out despite the dark – they were so close to me, in vague silhouette against the white masonry.

'No need trying to run away, you bastards,' I shouted at them. 'You're dead.'

I must have been mad. In a way, I was: suddenly crazed by yet another stressful event in my life, I was being someone else.

In the kitchen, immediately below the window they were about to force, I had a battery of kitchen knives I'd brought from home: I'm a keen and not unproficient cook, and there are certain implements and utensils I like to have about me when I travel. The knives, of beautifully tempered steel and furnished with handsome wooden handles and brass studs, were Spanish knives which I'd bought in Albacete some years before. They were all kept permanently and murderously sharp. I turned on all the lights of the apartment, strode straight to the kitchen and selected, without much procrastination, the one I always used for carving a good cut of beef. Its blade was almost nine inches long. I loved the feel of it in my hand.

Back outside, I saw from the balcony that the trio were making swift progress away, nimble as chamois, along the same contour level as the apartment.

'I'm coming after you,' I yelled. 'You can't escape.'

My shouts alerted the Warboys. By the time I'd taken the steps four at a time and reached the street, Gavin was on the pavement. I ran uphill towards him, flailing about with the knife. I was gasping, woefully unfit. He was unperturbed by my demeanour but instantly enraged when he knew what had happened.

'The cheeky buggers! That's the fourth time this month we've had break-ins up here. Had they got inside?'

'All but.'

'Come on! There's only one way they can go.'

Gavin's car was parked facing downhill. I assumed he would go forward and follow the curve of the 9-shaped street down, round and up to the pool, then along the dirt lorry-track which led to the downhill path on the far side of the gulch – the only viable escape route to Marbella for the intruders.

What he did, before either of us had closed the doors, was to put the car into reverse and propel it screaming and whining backwards up the very steep hill, violently lurching from side to side with the doors sagging on their hinges and straining wide open. The vehicle must have looked and sounded like some monstrous, extinct land-bird. When I was thrown forward against the windscreen, I might well have disembowelled myself with the blade. We stopped where the street levelled out, with smoke billowing.

'That'll be the clutch burning,' I said.

The doors slammed shut as we shot into forward gear and got up to fifty through the dust.

'We'll call the Bardots,' said Gavin. 'I don't fancy the odds, two against three. Not with gippos.'

The Bardots were the Spanish Sloanes who owned the developing estate. They had vast tracts of land elsewhere in Andalusia, wine country: father Bardot and two sons, one of whom reminded me of Prince Charles.

'How do you know they're gipsies?'

'Burglars round here always are.'

We skidded to a halt outside the Bardot villa. Gavin left me to wait in the car. Guard dogs were barking and snarling not far out of reach. The knife blade picked up the porch light. I stowed it on the dashboard shelf. Gavin was soon back.

'The Bardots'll chase up towards Istán. We'll do the lorry tracks and then go downhill. We're more likely to catch 'em than they are.'

'Why?'

'Because they're gippos. No gippos in Istán.'

'So it's still two against three?'

For about half an hour we drove furiously up and down dirt tracks and then down the Marbella road, taking blind corners at silly speeds, like Hollywood cops. What we were doing was daft: all the burglars had to do, I said, was lie low in the underbrush until we'd all had enough and went home.

'True enough.'

Back in Cerros del Lago, we met up with the Bardots. We all decided we had indeed had enough. The Bardots went home. Gavin and I remained chatting in his car for a short while. Then, on the point of saying goodnight, I saw three dim lights descending the path of the rabid dogs. There was no sound.

'That'll be them,' I said. 'Mopeds. Freewheeling.'

Gavin got Vicky to call the Bardots once more. And so the chase began again down the hairpins. We were a good half-way down to the coast road before we picked up their rear lights:

small motor-bikes are better adapted than cars for negotiating tight bends in the dark. They were in single file, with fifty yard spaces between them.

'We'll make do with the one at the back,' said Gavin. 'Ready?'

I took hold of the knife with the grip not of the carver, palm on top, but of the stabber, palm underneath the handle. Then, as Gavin overtook the rearmost rider, I flung open my door. We cut in, squealingly braked, and the gipsy — I could see at once that he was a gipsy — was caught astride his bike on the narrowest of verges. He had the car on one side of him and a long and painful knobbly drop the other. He was about eighteen, craven, scared out of his wits.

I had no business to threaten him as I now did; no need to bully him with words or weapons. I am a peaceable man normally, hating all forms of violence. But something of scum rose in me and made me terrify the gipsy lad while we waited for Bardot to come down the hill.

'Move one millimetre and I'll slit your throat,' I said. And I almost wished he had, so that I could. I have very often re-lived those minutes. I like to believe that, if it had come to an attempt on his part to escape, I would have been both cowardly and soft-hearted, and seen him go, and laughed afterwards at my impotence to act or even to behave like a responsible citizen.

Gavin was splendid, cool but unthreatening, whereas I had expected him to be crass.

'What's your name, son?'

'Manolo.'

'Where do you come from?'

'Monda.'

'Brothers and sisters?'

'Many.'

'Why do you steal?'

'To eat. *Hombre!*'

I felt no pity at all for him. Perhaps I was drained of the last drop of my compassion. He stood astride his bike, his gipsy head of thick, tousled hair wildly framed against the sky by the crook of a pomegranate tree; irrationally, I hated him.

Whether or not I'd have stuck the knife into him if he'd tried to make a break for it is something I shall never be sure about. On a very few occasions in my life I have been seduced by the prospect of imminently shed blood, whether my own or an adversary's. Once, on a building site, I came close to decapitating a tormenting foreman with a shovel. And once, miserably drunk and loveless, I put a cartridge into my single-barrel shotgun, cocked the trigger, walked out into my frost-filled garden and had the end of the barrel exactly round my Adam's-apple before tears welled and sobered me from reaching for the trigger. Such events are conjured up, unwelcome, from time to time by some shred of detail of daily experience: hearing the crunch of a shovel driven into gravel, feeling the first cold snap of autumn outside my back door. For the rest of my life, I suppose, the sight of pomegranates will remind me of a bend in the road between Cerros del Lago and the coast where, in a volatile interim, I might have been capable, if not of murder, then of inflicting very serious bodily harm. As it was, the Bardots arrived in their Mercedes and took charge of the gipsy boy and took him to the police station. I was driven back up the hill, where I went indoors, drank a tumbler of brandy, put my carving knife away with its innocent siblings, and went to bed.

The incident sent a *frisson* through the community. The news had probably been spread by the Bardots' servants, a nice old pair who did odd jobs for other residents in their free time. Next morning immediately after breakfast was chosen by a genial maintenance team to come and fix electricity meters in Sally's apartment. (Until now, electricity had been *gratis*.) Not realising that I spoke Spanish, the two men enacted a wonderfully lunatic mime of a savage knife-fight for my benefit while I did my spinsterish clearing-up of crumbs and the marmalade jar. It did me good to have my leg pulled; further, their antics were realistic enough to make me realise how foolhardy I'd been the night before: suppose the three young gipsies had come swarming over the balcony railings? And suppose they and their friends from Monda intended to come back mob-handed some time, when the dust had settled, and give me an individual lesson in the special, surgical skills of Romany knife-play? The thought made me shudder. However, as I made my way up to the pool it was gratifying to receive waves and smiles from two of my near neighbours, the wives, respectively, of a bank manager and a doctor; also, an invitation to dinner from a couple called Finch. They were sitting on their patio as I went past; I'd not seen them before, and I assumed they were holiday tenants.

'Oo, noo,' said Mrs Finch from under a straw hat which sported a band of little red woollen donkeys. 'We are the ooners.'

'Just about, still!' said her husband: not quite ruefully but in the manner of someone out on a disappointing spree and determined, come what may, to get his money's worth.

We chatted over the gate for ten minutes, sizing each other up. He was looking tired; old, I guessed, before his time, and in a detectable wig as well as a permanent state of worry. She had probably once been mightily attractive, and there was a last trace of flirtatiousness in her smile and in the way she pursed her lips to let her vowels have grudged access to the outside air. The Finches, though owning the apartment, seldom had the chance to use it, they told me: a fortnight in summer, a week in winter, maybe a short break over Easter if funds ran to it. The rest of the time it either lay empty or was rented out by the week, 'But oonly to naice people we knoo, of course.' They'd bought it out of their careful savings as a place to retire to, one distant day if they kept their health; but retirement, in the form of redundancy, was now all too likely to come several years before they'd expected. Jimmy Finch was a highly skilled electronics engineer with a company now threatened with being taken over by an international group. Highly skilled or not, he would have to accept being laid off and replaced by a younger man. And, at his age, he could entertain few prospects of finding a comparable job. They'd have to sell the apartment;

and, with the property market sluggish, they would probably finish up out of pocket. Their story was a template for many such victims of Mrs Thatcher's vision for England: apparent prosperity and the chimera of unlimited opportunity which, a promise betrayed, swiftly led to disappointment and disillusionment.

'And then there'd be all this furniture to dispose of. I was just saying to Josie, it'd be a favour if burglars came and took the lot one night. Collect the insurance. One problem less.'

'There will be noo more burglars, Jimmy. Mr Walker has freetened them all awee!'

'Oh – you've heard about that, have you?'

'Ay saw you mayself with the knaif.'

'We thought it'd be nice if you had a meal with us and told us all about it. This evening suit you?'

'There's not much to tell.'

'Come anyway. Sixish OK?'

I went and swam my mile, ungraciously pondering whether a few hours of generously offered (and, frankly, much yearned-for) company would be worth the risk of the kind of tedium which, once over, might leave me more dispirited than ever. What I needed was a stimulating boozing companion – a Vernon Scannell, a John Ormond – not suburban small-talk and tales of evaporating dreams. Another time, I could have been their good and sympathetic listener, but now the rest of the world was overdrawn on the bank of my patience and compassion. I had told the Finches almost nothing of myself, wanting to avoid lengthy explanations of my recently changed circumstances. I would just as soon keep it that way: but after a few drinks I would, as likely as not, pour my heart out and be, myself, the purveyor of boredom. They hallooed when, coming back from the pool, I passed their door, and I felt ashamed of what now seemed less like self-pity than an insufferable and overweening arrogance. They were kind, pleasant people; and despite Josie's gentility, which was attached to her personality as unconvincingly as her husband's hairpiece to his pate, they were, otherwise, genuine as bread.

I kept Spanish mealtime hours – three o'clock *comida*, ten o'clock *cena*. During that languorous afternoon I ate only black olives and some cubes of spiced *chorizo*, so as not to be too full for an early English supper. Like Auden, who found (in his poem, 'On the Circuit') *A change of mealtime utter hell*, I found myself full of the anxious thought: *What will there be to drink?*

And by five, appalled and engulfed by the panic of embarking upon a possibly dry evening (or, worse than dry, moderately moist; or, worse even than that, as much as one liked of some coloured, cloying concoction from an interesting bottle) I decided to snatch a few analeptic swigs of the excellent, if rough, Montilla I'd bought loose in a five-litre plastic container in Istán. By six (still thinking of Auden) I was ready for *one more audience I shall not see again.*

I took a bottle of *Gran Sangre de Toro* and a signed copy of one of my books to leave as a thank-you gift. The table was furnished not only with expected doileys but, propitiously, also with wine glasses. I gave Jimmy the book and handed the wine to Josie. 'Bull's Blood,' I said, hoping to startle her. She said I shouldn't have, then: 'Ay do soo hoop noo blood was shed last naight.'

I gave a flat account. Then Jimmy said: 'I've read this book. Did you really write it?'

He gave a summary of the book's subject matter as though he were a schoolboy showing that he'd done his homework thoroughly. I was flattered, but then Jimmy wanted to quiz me about my life as an author. I was having none of that.

'Do you have a job, Josie?'

'Oo, yes. Aim in Keetering.'

'Where's that?' Somewhere in Northampton, I thought, trying not to laugh. But no, if Josie were in catering, there was every chance of a good meal.

'At Jimmy's pleece.'

'That's a huge outfit. There must be hundreds and hundreds to feed at lunchtime.'

'Oo, yes. A quait large responsibility.'

I gathered from this that she was in charge of the entire

enterprise. I had a vision of her in a well-ordered office, with a secretary, having to deal with dockets and delivery-notes, invoices, menus, chefs and washers-up, cleaners, Health and Safety regulations, storerooms full of King Edwards and cans of bully beef.

'It must be an interesting job.'

'Oo, yes.'

'Quite stressful, though, at times?'

'Moost.'

'What exactly do you do?'

'Ay teek in the Managing Dairector's luncheon. On a tree.'

Jimmy noticed that there was a little smoke emanating from under the grill. We were having pork chops, on top of which Josie had spread a layer of, I guess, sage and onion bound in breadcrumbs. They were on fire. When they came to the table, the flames had subsided but the bread mixture was becoming its ashes, like the last gleeds in a grate. Had we been eating at twilight, the chops would have made a pleasing glow, now red, now white, now red again. It was a meal that would stay long in the memory.

By the time I left, full of chops and chips, trifle and much more wine than I'd dared expect, I'd told the Finches about my bereavement. It helped me, to do that. Soon, perhaps, I should be able to tell myself all about it, too – not omitting the unpalatable details, like the bits of gristle and burned discards I'd left on the side of my plate.

'At any rate,' said Jimmy, as I was leaving, 'from now on, you'll be able to do just what you like with your life. Live it up a bit. Your worries are over.'

THREE

I FILLED jugs and vases with red and white carnations. On a large pottery roundel, I piled oranges and lemons into a high pyramid. The apartment, with its vivid, David Hockney lines and colours, was resplendent when I left for Malaga airport to meet my daughter Susan. Her visit had been arranged at short notice: a few evenings before, I had rung from some desperate bar in San Pedro to tell her of my loneliness, and had been touched by her willingness to book as early a flight as possible.

I felt better as soon as I drove down the mountain, cheered by its immediate, golden, bearable beauty. Broom was in cascading yellow flower; seeding thistle-heads were encrusted with goldfinches. Below, along gulleys and ravines, fully-opened oleanders made sometimes straight and sometimes zigzag markers for the now dried-up water-courses. It was only late May, but already summer was high. I wound down the windows, selected a tape of *sevillanas* and let them rip at maximum volume. Just before leaving England, not so long before, I had walked in bluebell woods near Elgar's cottage in Sussex. There, a mottling sunshine had lain across cool lakes of flowers; blues, yellows, the delicately pararhyming light greens all but unknown in southern Spain. I would not have wanted to be back there now, contending with the insuperable beauty of beeches and windflowers and violet-strewn paths and black-berry lanes where Lorna and I had spent countless blithe hours with our children during their growing up. The great cello concerto would forever be thrumming among the branches and brambles and quilted velvet moss for me there, within yards of where it had been written; and, whereas I had once been able to luxuriate in the music's deep, *rubato* melancholy, (I being still young and detached from tragedy) the heart-breaking melodies – and the countryside of Downland and Weald I loved so profoundly – would have proved an unbearable torment: reminders, too acutely poignant, of stolen times of happiness amid a span of life whose dominant themes I now knew to be pain and sadness. Had I been in those woods again and found some late, pale primroses, I would have seen a darker yellow in the depths of the flowers: that terrible sallow of the complexion of the dying. I had looked at this sinister colour for too long, too lately. It was not to be countenanced again. Not yet.

Nor was I ready for remembering our happy times together:

> *Nessun maggior dolore*
> *Che ricordarsi del tempo felice*
> *Nella miseria.*

Dante's lines say it precisely: there is no greater grief than to recall a time of happiness when in misery. I needed not England but the foreign place I was in; its primary colours, terrific heat, light by which you could trace the veins in the gauze of a fly's wing; nothing in a minor key, no nuances, no subtle mistiness of a morning or evening when memories of unrepeatable pleasurableness, and of long, and long-ago, satisfactions, trouble the air breathed and sighed by mourners.

The French air traffic controllers were on a go-slow: it would be a long wait before Susan's plane touched down. I parked the car, crossed the railway tracks and went to the Lima café. It was the sort of rough-and-ready place where taxi-drivers and airport personnel loiter, playing uproarious games of cards to an incessant, obscene, blasphemous and cackling recitative. Outside, there was a ramshackle *parral* of vines and climbing roses, with iron tables and chairs. I ordered a carafe of wine and prepared to sit out the time in the half-shade.

★

It was something I'd done before, I remembered: just six days short of four years before, to be precise.

On that occasion, I had been waiting for Lorna's flight to arrive. She was going to spend a fortnight with me during my three months of travelling to research my book about Spain. In much the same way I had sat at the same table, drinking, picking at olives and peanuts, watching planes take off and land. And in much the same way now, I spilt some red wine on the white tablecloth.

The small spot of blood on a pillow had been all but forgotten by then. Five years had passed. When Lorna arrived, I took her to the simple hotel in Antequera where I had been holed up for a day or two, typing up notes. I had arranged a special dinner of her favourite foods, large prawns and straw-berries, then we went to the lively *feria*, and afterwards we made love, as we were to do every night of our tour of Andalusia, until we had to come back to Malaga for her flight home. That afternoon, too, the waiting hours were spent on the terrace of this same Lima café, under the terrace arbour. We were not overjoyed at the prospect of having to part again for another two months, but she was apparently fit and well, and we had not the slightest sense of time running out. Our lives would endure until the years not just of our grandchildren but of our great-grandchildren.

The spilt wine in front of me gradually spread its stain. I was transfixed by it. I thought of how the cancer must then have already begun opening in her head, the bud of a dark, diabolical rose.

After her first operation in 1978, when a small tumour was removed from the bone of the nose, the consultant declared himself confident of having caught the trouble in time. For a couple of years, she had three-monthly check-ups; for two and a half years more, six-monthly ones. 'There'll be no need to come back again for a full twelve months, if all's well next time,' he said after the last of these. It seemed as though she'd had a total remission, nothing less than we had felt entitled to expect: for at the first consultation, after the blood on the pillow, he had said that the chance of the malignancy recurring was remote; furthermore, because cancers in the head were slow-growing, it would probably be 'many years before it showed itself again', if ever it did. And when you are in your mid-forties, 'many years' puts you forward into unimaginable old age.

During the autumn after my summer's travels, I noticed how she kept dabbing at her nose with paper handkerchiefs; and when I examined these in the bin, I saw that they were flecked with red – the flecks scarcely as big as the freckles which appeared on her cheeks in warm weather. The next check-up at the Ear, Nose and Throat Department revealed that all was not well. Moreover, the seat of the problem had shifted, and was no longer the concern of an E.N.T. specialist. Her notes were passed to the Maxillo-Facial Unit. During the next weeks I drove her to various hospitals; biopsy followed biopsy, blood test followed blood test, X-ray followed X-ray, examination followed examination. Christmas was approaching when the results were all known. The M.F.U. consultant told us that a considerable part of her upper jawbone would have to be removed, and this, the sooner the better. We drove home in almost silence, neither of us finding anything to say.

The horrible fact hovered over the house like an evil bird; it infiltrated every room like a scarcely detectable gas, tainting our food, impregnating our clothes. The big, rosy apple of our life had been crudely split open and was browning over.

That Christmas Eve was my parents' Golden Wedding anniversary. Lorna decided that the celebration party should go ahead in our house, exactly as planned; none of the guests need know about her operation until nearer the time it was to occur. She completed a task she had set herself just before the series of exploratory tests had begun: the compilation of a fat album of photographs – a special present for her parents-in-law: snaps from nearly every one of their fifty years of marriage; them- selves, their children and their grandchildren. It was a long, time-consuming labour of love. Evening by evening I watched her arranging photographs on a page, writing captions for them, inscribing dates with a gold ink felt-tip pen; and I hoped that she was totally absorbed and not brooding on what was to come. I was glad, then, to see her busy preparing bedrooms, cooking, putting up decorations, making lists of things to do, things to buy. She baked a two-tier anniversary cake, covered tables with white cloths and set out cutlery and chinaware. Now and then she would pause, touch a place above her right cheek-bone, rub at her nose with a tissue. At midday on Christmas Eve the house was full of people. We had always enjoyed observing family ceremonials like this: special events, memorable rituals usually occurring in our house rather than elsewhere, not only because it was the roomiest and because it was old and characterful, or because I was the elder son, but – perhaps most importantly – because Lorna was a most dutiful, assiduous and competent wife, mother, daughter, daughter-in-law and friend, the responsible hub round whom the rest of the family revolved; and she always had her eye on the calendar so that birthdays and anniversaries would be not only anticipated but carefully planned for. She, it was, in her quietly unassertive way, who made things happen. Once again, she had brought everyone together: my parents and hers, our children and their partners, my brother and his family, as well as a couple of my parents' friends. Above the hubbub I heard one of the latter say of us, 'It's a wonderful time for all of them.' It must have seemed so. Apart from having the Golden Wedding to celebrate, our daughter Margaret had just qualified as a nurse, the others seemed to have launched happy and successful careers and I had a series of plays very soon to be shown on BBC Television. 'And doesn't everybody look well?' I heard the same voice say. The gold-wrapped presents were opened and the cake was cut and my father made a one-sentence speech and Lorna took the photographs necessary to complete the commemorative album.

Then it was Christmas itself; and when Christmas was finally over, and the children had all gone and we were left on our own to talk as best we could about the operation, Lorna had her heart attack.

She sat on a kitchen stool, first gently rocking, staring, as though cataleptic; but then she was violently doubled over by a stabbing spasm of chest pain. I telephoned for her doctor, though she said I need not, it was nothing at all to worry about. In a cold sweat of not knowing what to do, I could neither watch or look away while she suffered. I stood shivering in another room while the doctor was talking to her. I called for an ambulance when I was asked to do so. I brought her hat and coat and scarf and waited, preposterously helpless, until I heard the ambulance bell growing louder and saw its urgent lights flashing through the curtains. I watched as she was carried out on a stretcher under a menacing red blanket, and slammed the front door shut behind me. I sat beside her and held her hand while the bell rang and the lights kept flashing and the ambulance man kept up a running commentary of comforting words and reassurances all the way to the Accident and Emergency entrance. There was an hour-long series of examinations, the comings and goings of various doctors and nurses in different uniforms and insignia of rank, and I watched disturbing wires being attached to her and learned what the letters E.C.G. meant while a long, needle-like pen traced the peaks and troughs and intermediate serrations of her heart-beat. A kindly staff nurse suggested I should go home and pack a case with night clothes and a toilet bag. It would give me something useful to do, she said.

There was nothing useful to do except cure her heart and her poor head; but I did as I was told and called a taxi.

I was frightened by the look of the empty house, the kitchen chair with an old cardigan draped over its back, the washing-up not done. When wild imaginings about what might be happening to her grew rampant, I coughed and retched from terror and hawked and spat, trembling, into the sink. I forced myself to think of the smell of lemons, the sight of apple blossom. It was unthinkable that she should die. But suppose she did? Suppose she already had? Suppose she had wanted me with her? What would she have thought of me for going home when I did? Not staying?

I had yet to learn how to deal with my squeamishness, my pointless fastidiousness. When I invaded the privacy of her chest of drawers, packed her intimate things, found out where the towels and spare flannels were, I entered a dimension of our marriage which was strange to me – the locked wing of a mansion whose inheritor has come across its rusted key.

I drove back to the hospital along empty night roads. By now she was in the Intensive Care Unit, and I was not allowed to see her. I sat outside until morning light grew stronger than the neon, and the rexine-covered tubular chairs in the waiting-room took on their other, daytime identity: furniture to be sat upon rather than slumped in or slept along. I could stay there as long as I liked, I was told, but it would be better to get some proper rest. They would phone me if I was needed, they said; so I went home again and drank some whisky and fell asleep on the sofa by the telephone.

A peremptory astoundment through the house, it woke me at mid-morning. Her condition was stable; I could visit.

The Intensive Care Unit unnerved me: a hushed, twilit, sci-fi cave containing paraphernalia beyond my understanding and a few, scarcely visible, stertorous breathers of whom one was my wife. A VDU screen flickered its line of viridian green scribblings, erasing itself as it went and re-starting its progress left to right, over and over again, proof of her life continuing. I found her cold hand and held it gently, wanting mine to be gently squeezed; and immediately cursed myself for selfishly seeking reassurance instead of offering it. So then I squeezed very gently, and whispered her name; and she opened her eyes and spoke mine. I had not lost her. The hospital gown, with its tie-up tapes, looked a contemptible thing, it made an even more pathetic object of her. I told her I had brought her nightgown, that all would be well, that she was being looked after by good people, that they would only let me stay a few minutes more, that she must try and sleep again. She closed her eyes when I asked her to and when I judged her to be asleep I got up and left. I thought, She has known what it is like to be dying, and I have guessed what it would be like to be deprived of her for ever.

I had witnessed a kind of resurrection. After letting the rest of the family know what had happened, I tried to be calm and take stock. It seemed more than likely (after talk with the doctors) that the heart attack had been brought on by the anxiety of contemplating a particularly unthinkable operation. It would mean having a hole made through the side of the head as well as the removal of the diseased part of the jawbone. Her life, and her way of life, would be permanently changed. Without much doubt her good looks would be seriously impaired. In middle age she had been acquiring that second bloom of beauty which fair women take on after their children have grown up and further childbearing is no longer a possibility: when, finally, all other gynaecological problems are done with, too. (She had had a long series of these, culminating in a hysterectomy.) And what would she be able to eat? She had always enjoyed a hearty appetite; who could relish the prospect of a diet of pap? After my return from Spain, we had experienced, as couples often do, a new falling-in-love of an unsentimental – but none the less romantic – nature. The surprise of this unselfconscious rediscovery of each other had led to a prolonged new courtship and honeymoon-within-marriage. It was enhanced by the sense of freedom that might be enjoyed now that our parental duties were accomplished: we could do as we chose in the house, come and go as we pleased – subject only to Lorna's needing to keep an eye on her increasingly infirm parents in the annexe. Knowledge of the operation made smithereens of aspects of our fancied future. Sensuous meals followed by sensual dalliance were a dream cleanly incised by the notion of the surgeon's saw. Disappointment and disenchantment brought on her attack as much as anxiety, and the stress and rush of the Golden Wedding party had doubtless hastened its occurrence. As ever, she had done what she considered was expected of her, and only when her tasks were well and truly finished had she allowed herself to stop staving off what had to happen, sometime, with her heart. With all the craven wisdom of the eternal weak man after the event, I vowed never again to let her be so overwhelmed if I could help it. I was going to look after her, without let-up, always, and my love for her would be more than the commonplace love of the lover.

Two days later, she was removed by ambulance to St George's Hospital in south London. I found her sitting up in bed. She had been able to brush her hair and make up her face. I cried, seeing her as alive as she had used to be, with a little colour in her face and a propensity to smile. 'I'm going to have to learn how to do easy things again,' she said, 'like walking upstairs.'

First, though, she was permitted to walk only the length of the ward. After a few days, she was able to take my arm and slowly promenade along the central aisle. We must have looked like an ancient couple taking the evening air along a village street. Most of her fellow patients were old and confined to bed; but many of them were of our age or younger. Some sat in chairs at the end of the bed with the weary air of peasants watching the passing scene from their cottage threshold; others shuffled this way and that, carrying small black boxes which proved to be heart monitors. Lorna told me a little about every one of them: this one was a milkman, father of six; that one was a misanthropic spinster; another was a young nurse who had been at work in this very same mixed ward when her heart attack began. Each one had some kind of heart or respiratory disease.

'And each one is here because of smoking,' she said, as she settled back into bed, beginning to feel tired. 'The chap in the bed by the door has got emphysema on top of his heart trouble. He used to get through eighty a day, and he says he can't and won't stop, whatever they tell him. That's why he's in the end bed. It's not just for him to be close to the nurse's office – so that they can give him oxygen when he's gasping. No. It's so's he can nip out to the corridor for a crafty drag. He had his pace-maker fitted last week.'

I plumped her three pillows and arranged them in the way I'd learned by now: the three bars of a stubby letter A. Two of the nearby beds were occupied by patients who had had to have their legs amputated, their blood vessels having furred up.

'I'm really going to have to give up, you know,' she said.

'I'll help you, one way or another.'

'And the doctor told me today that I need a good three months to get over this business before – you know.'

'What?'

'Before I can take the operation. Anaesthetic. Everything.'

Our children arrived with their partners. The bed was strewn with presents and cards and flowers. It was a cosmetically cheery scene. I saw through their smiles to their worry.

'There's only supposed to be three visitors at a time,' I said sententiously. 'I'll go for a breath of fresh air.'

I daresay they heard the lie behind my words. What I was going for was a smoke. Outside, it was a slow snivel of end-of-January rain and shreds of sleety snow. For another three months at least that black bud in her head was going to open more of its hateful outer petals. It lay upon the bone of her skull, close to where the centre of her being was, and it could not be plucked out before her heart was properly mended. I scrabbled and scratched at the Cellophane wrapper round a new packet of twenty, my hands all of a cold tremble. When finally I got a cigarette between my lips, I found it difficult to select and strike a match; and when the match ignited, the wind blew it out at once. And the next one, and the next. By the time the cigarette was lit and I could draw on it, the paper was becoming sodden with the rain in the air and the wet off my hand, and it disintegrated in my fingers. I wanted to be back at the bedside straight away; but before I went inside, I found a litter bin and emptied my pockets of smoking materials. Apart from the new packet, there was an old one containing three cigarettes, some cheroots, two boxes of safety matches, a book-match from some restaurant and a lighter which needed re-filling with gas. I then pulled out the linings of my pockets and brushed them clean of fluff and tobacco shreds. By this deed, on the 31st of January 1984 – another anniversary to observe – I became a non-smoker.

My withdrawal symptoms had begun before I'd half completed the sixty-mile drive home; but, once indoors, I gathered up every ashtray in the house, smashed them and threw them out. Between visits to the hospital and teaching my classes, I laundered and ironed all the curtains, cleaned all the carpets and washed down the walls until the whole house smelt fresh and free of the foul and musty stink of smoke. By now, Lorna was able to take a flight of stairs gently; once or twice a morning, once or twice of an afternoon, getting stronger. We avoided talk of the future. As it was to turn out, she was to pretend, for everyone else's benefit, to take most of what remained of her life one day at a time. But doubtless she was incessantly laying down more and more strata of perturbation on to some chill inner core of fret. I was not bamboozled by her carefree demeanour when I was with her. I knew her too well. She might camouflage her fear, but her courage was not to be concealed. I could tell she was filling much of her day and night thinking about the ordeal to come. I was. Sometimes it triggered in me an uncontrollable shivering spell, so frozen was I in my anxiety. One afternoon, after we had climbed the day's quota of steps in the hospital, I started a trembling fit at the sight of a middle-aged woman patient being wheeled swiftly past on a trolley, accompanied by a scuttling covey of nurses. The woman had tubes inserted in both nostrils; above her, swaying on hooks, were containers of the various fluids needed to sustain her life. The way she looked, the urgent way she was being hustled along the ridged concrete floor on rattling wheels, she could not survive the night. Now, remarkable as this must seem, at the age of forty-nine I had still not seen a dead body; and, in that instant, I had the gruesome, involuntary premonition that Lorna's could be the first one I should see.

'Why are you shivering, love?' she asked me, gripping my arm tighter.

'Tobacco deprivation,' I fibbed. 'Takes me like that now and then. Like an alky with the shakes.'

'You see worse than that in here,' she said. She knew me too well, too.

'No,' I persisted, 'I get this kind of pressure across the shoulder blades. And light-headedness. I get giddy.'

'You don't have to stop just because I have to.'

'Yes I do. We'll manage. Find things to take our minds off it.'

So we talked on about a life without cigarettes; but our unmentionable sub-text was how, mutually, to pretend to ignore the dread. By some alchemy of intuition, we were able to make a contract which bound us, in future, not to mention the operation; or what ghastly deterioration might occur during the three-month delay caused by the heart attack. My daughter Margaret was to tell me how, at this time, they had talked about the matter openly. 'I'm not intending to go through with it,' Lorna had said; and Margaret, wearing her nurse's cap, had replied, 'Well, you know really that you're going to have to.' After a pause, her mother had said, 'Yes, I know I do. Because if I don't, I'll die.' She probably thought she would not survive whether or not she had the operation; in which case, it could be said that it would have been wise if I'd initiated a dialogue similar to Margaret's: but we suborned each other towards a policy of not alluding to that which ultimately could not be avoided. It was a *modus vivendi* which suited our book. We both knew what we were up to. We weren't daft.

So it was that, after her discharge from St George's, we embarked upon a largely unplanned programme of escapism.

I had no classes to teach on Fridays or Monday mornings. We were able to get away for long weekends, sometimes leaving on Thursday afternoons and not returning until an hour or so before my new week's duties began. Four nights away out of seven: she had a horror of being at home, where the reminders were. We stayed at hotels in beautiful cities: Bristol, Canterbury, Cheltenham, Bath; we visited zoos such as Marwell, Lympne and Longleat, and Bird Parks and Butterfly Parks. When the warmer weather of spring began, we went to seaside resorts like Weston-super-Mare and Dover; we toured great houses and National Trust sites whenever we came upon them; we inspected wayward museums containing dolls, musical-boxes, vintage cars; we rode on miniature trains and aerial runways, sat on steam-rollers and open-top buses; we crossed to France for a day-trip by hovercraft, refusing the hostess's blandishments to buy duty-free cigarettes; we looked at handsome parish churches, and Belloc's windmill, and antique shops, formal gardens, observatories, ancient ships, cathedrals, sawmills, exhibitions of advertising and packaging. We would sit in the car to eat a picnic lunch, gazing through the windscreen at wonderful vistas of landscape: the Chilterns, the Cotswolds, the Kentish Weald, the Vale of the White Horse. Sometimes, on a Sunday afternoon, we might be only an hour's drive from home, but none the less we would look for one more nondescript room where, after we'd eaten an un-satisfactory meal out, we could lie on the bed doing *The Times* crossword puzzle and, when this was completed or abandoned, watch whatever happened to be on television. When morning came, and there was no option but to make tracks for home, there would still be opportunities for further procrastination; a shopping arcade to inspect, a cup of coffee to drink, guide-books and maps of the local area to select. The car's compart-ments were crammed with town plans, leaflets and booklets called What There Is To Do in this place or that.

But, whatever we did to disregard it, the time elapsed: four months, not three. The Thursday came when we had to pack a small case and drive to the hospital. Our route lay through unremarkable farmland; field after field of gaudy yellow rape. I sensed that she was gazing out of the passenger window, avoiding my eye, with the air of one looking her last on all things lovely. Many times in the past I had taken her to hospital; never before, though, had there been such unspoken foreboding. It had the effect of pushing us apart, as lines of force do between like poles of a magnet. She withdrew into a carapace of private fortitude. No matter what sentimentalists say, there are occasions when – however much we love or are loved – we know ourselves to be ultimately alone.

By the evening visiting hour, she had made herself at home in the ward. There was nothing strange for her about hospitals, nothing the nurses could tell her that she didn't already know. A pragmatist, she had spent the intervening hours between being admitted and my arrival arranging her things so that they would be easily accessible when she arrived back from theatre. She had made lists of jobs I should do, items to buy, people to phone. I had bought her a jolly-faced clown to sit on the corner of her bedside cabinet. It wore a pink polka-dot pyjama suit and a tall, conical hat with pom-poms, and it smiled cheerfully with a wide, U-shaped mouth, red nose and black little eyes. You could place him in various attitudes: cross-legged, or Humpty-Dumpty style with legs dangling, or with one knee bent and the other out straight, like a yogi. He became, instantly, a kind of emblem of her obduracy: nothing at all in common with those doe-eyed, anthropomorphised soft toys which sap the spirit.

'Nice and colourful – better than flowers,' I said. 'He'll be there when you wake up.'

'Was it expensive?'

'Of course not. Who cares?'

'You ought to care. We've been spending so much, lately. All those hotels and eating out. Don't forget to feed the cat.'

'No.'

'The papers need paying.'

'We'll have a proper holiday when you're up to it.'

'Maybe, one day.'

'Don't be glum. This time tomorrow, the worst bit'll be over.'

'I'll never be able to crunch into a stick of celery again.'

'Of course you will.'

'I won't.'

'You will. I promise.'

It was a fatuous thing to say, and it made her cry. There was nothing I could promise her in respect of her illness. There was also nothing I could say of genuine comfort: nothing in which the two of us could believe. The only solace was in a shared silence; that, and the physical contact of an arm-in-arm walk to the lift and a long embrace, and wry, forced smiles when the lift doors closed between us. In the carpark, I looked up at the window by her bed. She was standing there, waving, like a traveller at the taffrail of a departing ship.

She phoned to say goodnight.

'You didn't forget the cat?'

'No. She's all right. Did they give you any dinner?'

'Mince and mash. But a nice crisp apple.'

'I had a chop.'

'I get nothing else now. No breakfast.'

The pips went. I all but said her time was running out. 'I love you,' I said; and she was able to say the same before the line cut.

She phoned to say good morning.

'You forgot to take my case home.'

'Damn.'

'It's under the bed. I got told off.'

'I'll take it away this afternoon. Sorry. How do you feel?'

'A bit jittery. I'll be all right when they've come with the pre-meds. They're taking me down at half-past ten. Could be a longish job. You can phone at two o'clock. How are you feeling?'

'You can guess.'

'Don't worry. Thanks for my clown. I do love you.'

'Love you, too. Very much. See you soon.'

'Goodbye.'

The word, and the click of the phone, fetched me a savage back-hander.

Had it not been a Friday, I could have spent the morning in front of supine students, blathering about poetry. As it was, by half-past ten I was on my knees in the cathedral, superstitiously entreating the God I would not believe in. It was years since I had tried to pray. I had never been any good at it: but I tried again, there, then, because there was nothing more helpful for me to do, and nowhere better to do it. Like the persona of Larkin's great poem, I had tended to a cross of ground – though I knew the ghostly silt dispersed – because it was a serious house on serious earth. My unaccustomed knees soon hurt, but I stayed put. I watched a chivvying sexton getting rid of a party of Japanese. A minor cleric in a cassock did some arcane duty in the chancel. My words would not come. I looked to my left and saw the Arundel Tomb – the subject of another of Larkin's poems (one of the greatest love poems in the language, in my view) – surrounded by the *black, purgatorial rails* which Keats had put into another great poem about love, 'The Eve of Saint Agnes'. Many a time I had brought parties of students to look at the monument, pointing out the details of Larkin's imagery: blurred faces of the Earl and Countess, the armour, the little dogs at their feet, the way they held hands. Now, having found nothing to say to an inaccessible God, I felt for the first time the full significance of the final line. *What will survive of us is love.* Yes, I hoped it was true; but, as the penultimate line tells us, to believe this was only an 'almost-instinct' and it was only 'almost true'. How many times had Lorna and I lain together, side by side, with the knowledge of her cancer dividing us like the bolster in a low, music-hall joke, but then holding hands like those ancient stone effigies. Never mind if the line fell ever so slightly short of the Truth, the whole Truth, and nothing but the Truth, the last words of the poem said what I most wanted said at that moment. I closed my eyes and repeated it like a mantra. *What will survive of us is love. What will survive of us is love. What will survive of us is love.* Poetry was as close as I could get to prayer. It would have to do.

I walked to the easternmost end of the cathedral, behind the high altar. By now, I guessed, she would be in theatre. I lit a candle and pushed it on to an iron prong; then I put some money into a box and helped myself to a printed card the size of a bookmark. I read the words of the Prayer of St Richard:

> Thanks be to Thee, my Lord Jesus Christ,
> For all the benefits which Thou hast given me,
> For all the pains and insults
> Thou hast borne for me.
> O most merciful redeemer,
> Friend and Brother,

May I know Thee more clearly,
Love Thee more dearly,
And follow Thee more nearly.

My first radio play, 'The Final Miracle', had been based upon the question: who had been the very last person to make a pilgrimage to the Shrine of St Richard – there, where I was standing by my burning candle – hoping for a miracle? I had set the action long ago in time: some indeterminate period, perhaps the late seventeenth century. A craftsman carpenter with a 'wasting disease' is brought on a cart by his family all the way to Chichester from Droitwich – the Worcestershire town where St Richard himself had been born. The carpenter's wife, his daughter, his brother, and he himself, represent the various gradations of faith from simple, unshakeable peasant belief, through positive and negative agnosticism, to downright hostile atheism. At first, it looks as though the man has been cured; up in the watching-loft above the shrine, he manages to stand and walk unaided: but then he trips and tumbles down the steps of the rough ladder, and his neck is broken. In my heart, I discounted the efficacy of what I had come to do. Not to have done it, though, would have been somehow unwise.

Dylan Thomas, in a note to his *Collected Poems*, said, rather apologetically:

I read somewhere of a shepherd who, when asked why he made, from within fairy rings, ritual observances to the moon to protect his flocks, replied: 'I'd be a damn' fool if I didn't!' These poems with all their crudities, doubts, and confusions, are written for the love of Man and in praise of God, and I'd be a damn' fool if they weren't.

When I stepped from medieval penumbra into the candid light of twentieth-century day, I felt a momentary twinge of embarrassment about what I had done. My attempts at prayer and my superstitious ceremony had been interfused with crudity, doubt and confusion: but then, Hell, I thought; I'd have been a damn' fool, too, if I hadn't come and lit my candle

58

and tried my damnedest to will it to do its work. And when I phoned the hospital on the dot of two, and heard that Lorna was back in the ward and that all was 'satisfactory', I found myself saying thank you, aloud, into the air, and seeming to mean it.

Satisfactory: a word which, in the context of school reports and medical bulletins, means the precise opposite of its dictionary definition.

'Satisfactory' was woefully unsatisfactory, I discovered, when she had recovered enough to get out of bed and walk a little.

Unimaginable probings and incisions and excisions had taken place, I knew, inside her head. What I saw was the immediate and shocking effects of these dispositions: the horribly swollen right cheek, the bandaging, the plasters, the gamboge and purple bruising that seeped from under their edges to encroach into the residual health of her fair complexion. I found it very difficult to understand her speech: her vowels had few discernible consonants to split them into sense. She pointed to her face, made noises like those of an intelligent spastic. Unable to communicate, she quickly grew frustrated and enraged. Gradually, by taking her phrases and sentences more slowly and deliberately, she transmitted comprehensible messages. I wondered, in a new panic: was she always going to sound like this?

A nurse came along and said to me, 'Perhaps you'd be the best one to help her with the obdurator.'

I had never heard the word before. I had to have it explained. It was a prosthesis whose function was to close the hollow made by the removal of some of the bone of the jaw. It was a piece added to the upper part of the upper denture, and it required the acquisition of a new skill to fit it into place.

'I've tried, but I can't do it on my own. I can't.'

'I'll help you, love.'

'I can't face it again. It hurts like anything.'

'We'll have to try, though.'

'I want a bath first. Help me?'

59

'Love to.'

I pushed her in a wheelchair to the bathroom, and I locked us in so that we could cry in each other's arms with nobody to see us. Then I ran a bath for her, undressed her as tenderly as I had used to do when we were young lovers; and I soaped her flannel and washed as much of her face as I could see, and then her neck and shoulders, and then her breasts with my bare hands. For a few minutes more we were playful, half laughing and half weeping. And then I rinsed the soap away and helped her step out on to the bare tiles: it was a comfortless room. When I had dried her and sprinkled talcum powder, I helped her put on a clean nightgown I had brought from home. She put on her dressing-gown unaided. Gummily, having neither her top nor her bottom dentures in place, she smiled. She was grotesque, yet beautiful.

'You're going to be all right,' I said.

'Do you think so?'

'Let's have a go with that obdurator.'

A nurse brought in a kidney dish covered with a cloth. 'She'll soon get the hang of it. Just a matter of practice.'

'But it hurts so much.'

'Got to have patience, haven't we? Tell her, Mr Walker.'

Imagine a rough flint, such as you might pick off a flower-bed after rain; rough-edged, greyish, dirty-white. Imagine it, big as a Brazil nut, stuck to a denture. It was made of some kind of plaster composition, looking slightly granular to the touch.

'I can hardly get it into my mouth, let alone fixed in place.'

'You've done it once,' said the nurse.

'A och-och ich-ich-ich.'

'Come again?'

'The *doctor* fitted it.'

'He showed you how. It's a knack.'

'I'll never do it on my own.'

I put my arm round her; then picked up the obdurator with a paper tissue and put it in her hand. 'Please try,' I said, 'just for me.'

She tried, but gagged.

'Take your time, dear,' said the nurse. 'Nobody's going to rush you.'

The knack was, apparently, to push it first back so far, then sideways so far, then back again a few millimetres. 'Until it kind of clicks into place,' said the nurse. 'If you could do it once, you can do it again.'

'Another try?' I said.

She was holding it between thumb and forefinger. It still glistened with her spittle.

'Maybe if I take a deep breath first,' she said. She made a great effort to calm herself, breathing deeply, the way athletes do before putting in their best effort: in her day, she had been a superb swimmer, a County-standard hockey and tennis player. I thought of how she would prepare to serve, still and calm; and how she would toss the ball high and bring the racket in a wide, accelerating arc. So, now, concentrating, she rehearsed what had to be done: then did it, in one fluid, economical movement. An ace. She gripped my hand very tight.

'Hurrah!' I said.

However, it was not a triumphant smile on her face but the ambiguous grimace of seething pain.

'Splendid, my dear,' said the nurse. 'Again.'

'No, no. No more,' she said. 'Not now.'

'Just once more,' said the nurse. 'Now – before you forget how you did it.'

'Let her have a breather, for God's sake,' I said. I was sweating, full of an imagined, excruciating pain.

'Take it out again, there's a good girl.'

She did as she was told. Her eyes were watering. Taking it out was a knack, too. She held the obdurator above her head, like a conjuror showing he had nothing up his sleeve. Then she inserted it once more, removed it, put it back in the kidney dish.

'Now I'm going for a rest,' she said. 'And that's final.'

'Just put it back in place once more,' said the nurse.

'Leave her alone,' I said.

'Once it's back, it can stay put, you see. But it's really got to go back, so that things can shape and heal round it. The worst part's over. Just a question, then, of learning how to clean it. And everywhere round it. There's a special squirter arrangement to do that with. This is just a temporary obdurator. The permanent one's going to be a lot less clumsy and knobbly than this – more like an ordinary denture. Smoother. Smaller. So pop it back in, dear, and then I promise to leave you both in peace.'

★

I watched a plane in Air France livery coming in to land, and guessed it was my daughter's. I gave it ten minutes to taxi in, another ten to have the steps wheeled into place and its doors opened. By the time I'd finished my wine, paid my bill and strolled back to the Arrivals gate, I was able to see Susan through the screens.

She was one of the first through the barrier. It had never struck me before how closely she resembled her mother at that age. She grinned cheerily, put down her luggage and opened her arms for a hug.

'Hello, Old Bean, how are you?' She always called me Old Bean.

'Not too bad,' I said. 'Really glad to see you.'

'I've been thinking of mum.'

'So've I.'

FOUR

THEREAFTER, until the end of her stay, we seldom mentioned our grief. It was not yet the right time for me to speak my thoughts to my children, perhaps from the fear of saying the wrong thing or saying the right thing in the wrong way. Susan had her other sorrows: she had lost her partner, too, for her marriage had come to an end, and she still missed the baby of her miscarriage several years before.

One day, in San Pedro, we walked back to the spot where I had parked the car. It was missing. We stared at the empty space, first in astonishment, then in disbelief, then in outrage, then in helpless despair. We walked up and down the street, and the adjacent streets, wondering what we should do. We had left our valuables locked in the car; our papers, tickets, cheque books, credit cards, passports. We were dispossessed, and suddenly without identity. Then, on the point of going to the police station (and I had small faith in the efficacy of doing that) I saw the car. It was precisely where I had left it. I was astonished and incredulous again, but in a different way. How could it be there – the ghost of the car I had already accepted I should never see again? I felt foolish; outraged with myself, helpless to explain my mistake, in despair lest I should be going dotty. Of course, I had been seeking it in the wrong place. I all but wept with relief. The experience was the converse of a phenomenon which took place on several occasions during bereavement: when you had the momentary illusion that you might come across the lost loved one again in just such a

63

fashion; she was merely temporarily misplaced, waiting to be found again, with her own identity intact, as well as that large part of yours which she represented. Her space, though, had been permanently vacated. You were never in error about where she had been the last time you saw her. Quite often, as now, when we drove off with giggles of relief, I very nearly addressed Susan by her mother's name.

'Do you remember that time – oh, no.'

'Go on.'

'Nothing. You wouldn't know about it, of course. Silly me.'

'What?'

'Your mum once trailed round and round the wrong carpark looking for the old Morris Minor. It all turned out fine. Nothing to tell, really. These things happen.'

The genial old lady who kept a small corner shop in Istán took Susan to be my young wife.

'No! My daughter. My wife died very recently.'

'I'm sorry. Forgive me. Then no doubt your daughter will be looking after you from now on. I've looked after my brother ever since his poor wife died.'

'I'm sorry. When was that?'

'Forty years ago. A man needs a woman to look after him, doesn't he? How do you like Spain?'

'I love it. My second country.'

'And your daughter?'

'Very much. But it's different for me. I've spent a lot of time living here.'

'Where was that?'

'All over. Mainly in Castile.'

'Come – I have something to show you. Then we'll go and find Paco in the orchard.'

'But what about the shop?'

'Bah! Business can always wait. *Vengan!*'

She told me her name: Pilar. I told her ours: Eduardo and Susana. We shook hands, and I did a formal little bow for her. Outside, on the step, she locked the shop door with one of a large bunch of keys which hung on a plaited cord at her waist. She then led the way, ceaselessly chattering and laughing, waving back to hands and faces at windows.

'What was all that about?' Susan asked.

'I didn't catch all of it,' I fibbed. 'But we're off to see her brother.' As we progressed to the end of the village street, I thought of me looking after myself, alone, for as many as forty years. I could manage the practicalities. Lack of companionship would be the problem. Between the two women I now strolled beside, there was a cultural divide as deep as the chasm at Ronda. In my father's middle years – certainly my grand-father's – a widower in our family would have been taken in, as a matter of course, by an unmarried sister or daughter. The notion was as quaint in England, now, as a sepia photograph; as much a domestic bygone as a copper warming-pan.

Pilar took us into an old, half-empty, newly-renovated house. It was three storeys high, superbly equipped with a modern bathroom and kitchen. In her shop, one had been able to peep through a curtain at the living-room she and her brother shared; it was cosy in an old-fashioned, cluttered and comfortable style, all knick-knacks and bric-à-brac, much like a Victorian English parlour. This other property of hers – its fabric of whitewashed stone of a similar age as that of the shop, early eighteenth century – was partly furnished with attractive, expensive, clean-lined modern furniture. Pilar showed us every room on every floor, moving with surprising agility up and down the stairs.

'For our old age, you understand?'

'Ah – this is where you intend to retire to?'

'No, no, no! Retire? That's what happens when you fall and break your bones and they cart you off to the old folks' home. No. This is for pin money. We're going to rent it out. Perhaps you would be interested? Or your friends? No? Never mind. I couldn't live in a place like this either, but it seems to be what young people must have these days. Machines! Machines!'

Her last words, *máquinas! máquinas!* began the cackle which continued until we were outside and she had shut the front door behind us. If she was disappointed at not finding, in us, prospective paying tenants, she showed no sign of it.

The street petered out, to become first a cart track and then a footpath. After another fifty yards, Pilar took us through a gap in the dry-stone wall into a steeply-inclined field. At the bottom of this was a grove of mixed citrus trees with, here and there, a small patch of cultivated ground. The shade among the lemon trees, after the full heat of late-morning sun, was like a cool, moist flannel pressed to one's face. I could hear, but very faintly, the trickling of hidden water.

'Paco?' Pilar called out. 'Paco? Where's that brother of mine? Paco?'

'I'm coming. What's up?'

'Come and meet our guests.'

Paco had not been far away; but we had not seen him, so well was he camouflaged among the thin shafts of blinding light which penetrated the shadows of the orchard. He emerged into the clearing where we stood, a benign old upright mammal in a shaggy cardigan. He was carrying a draw-hoe. We shook hands. He took off his straw hat and wiped his head with a red handkerchief.

'My daughter and I admire your trees very much, sir,' I said. I indicated a particularly lovely one, whose dark green leaves shone as though lacquered, and on which the lemons had swollen prolifically, like a window display of toy rugby balls.

'Bah! I'll show you some real trees. Does the young lady like oranges?'

'He says, "Do you like oranges?"'

'Tell him, "Is the Pope a Catholic?"'

I did, and Paco laughed. He led us to some trees further off, a little higher up the slope. I could see the quietly flowing rivulet now. Paco had been drawing an irrigation channel down from some higher source, still out of sight. At the point he had reached before our arrival had interrupted him, the water was spreading in a wide, shining fan, wasting, steaming a little into rising clouds where midges and butterflies were hovering.

The old man pointed to a magnificent orange tree. Some of

the fully-ripened fruit were caught in a shaft of sunlight so that, instead of studding the foliage in an arbitrary scatter, they made an effect like an embroidered banner, an oriflamme to bedeck our small arena as for a medieval tourney.

'Take one of those,' said Paco. 'Take the best one you can find.'

I reached up and plucked one. It came with the stalk and a single leaf, and it sat plump and heavy on my hand, the lustre of its rind as delicate and slightly yielding to the fingertips as the skin of a young girl's face. It was an orange out of Eden, the pristine elaboration of God in the first flush of creation. Paco took it from me; and with a single stroke of his long-bladed knife, sliced it cleanly through its equator. He gave half to Susan and half to me.

'Eat it,' he said. And he drove his hoe with a splash into the welling channel and dragged it towards him, making a soggy shive slop from the iron.

Before I bit, I admired the stellated patterning revealed by the cut: the perfectly uniform white circle of pith within the zest, the abundance of succulent juice that could not but ooze, even without pressure. We found we could not proceed with delicacy. It was a fruit to be savaged, gulped at, drunk from, to tear from its skin with your incisors pulling back the half segments like Paco's draw-hoe tearing through his russet-coloured earth. When I had done, I guess my drooling chops must have looked like those of a dromedary after long quaffing at an oasis.

'Take as many as you like,' said Pilar. 'Oranges. Lemons.'

She gave each of us a plastic carrier-bag from her apron pocket. 'Fill them up! Fill them up!'

We were embarrassed to do what she said: more embarrassed still, not to.

'Fill them up! Fill them up!'

And so we began to pluck the fruit. We were clumsy. It was so easy to snap the slender twigs.

'Like this,' said Pilar.

As with the obdurator, there was a knack. You lifted the

fruit, taking its weight in your palm, then you twisted firmly and you had your prize. I half filled my bag, then watched Paco intent at his work. He was making exactly geometrical channels, parallel with each other; then these were linked, and the obedient water ran; and the sub-channels were conduits in their turn, back to the main furrows of irrigation. All the time, the precious liquid flowed almost soundlessly, but so full of playful sunlight that you wondered how it could be so mute.

Pilar took my bag from me and filled it almost full.

'You like apricots?'

'Yes. I used to grow peaches.'

Paco paused, hearing this. 'You have an orchard?'

'In my country we grow them under glass. My peaches had white flesh.'

'You don't grow them any more?'

'No.'

'You have a garden for vegetables?'

'Not now. Before,' I said. '*Antes.*'

'Yours is a cold country, right? Up there in the north. What could you grow?'

I ransacked my Spanish for the words. Most of the more common ones came easily: potatoes, onions, beans, lettuce. I had forgotten 'carrot'. I described what it was, an orange-coloured root, and Paco came up with my disremembered *zanhoria*. It became a parlour game: I would define what a radish was, or a loganberry, or a pumpkin; and Pilar and Paco would compete to see who could guess it first.

'A man needs a garden to look after,' Paco said, when I had run out of verbal invention.

He was the Spanish equivalent of old Jack Talbot, whom I thought of: at that moment, perhaps, tending the plot that had once so fulfilled me. I would never need to fill wheelbarrows full of fruit and vegetables again. The children were grown up, and I was alone. It would be marvellous, though, to have a few lemon trees, and some chickens, and a patch of salad crops, and a vine to give you shade and a dessert in summer. I would give away most of the eggs and lemons, of course, but I'd keep the cool air of the *parral* and the grapes. I began to think of an alternative life, my doppelgänger snipping and gathering. It was a romantic notion, but not impossibly so.

'You have a paradise here,' I said. 'I envy you.'

'A little of everything,' said Paco. 'Enough for your needs. It's something to do with your life.'

'The apricots,' said Pilar. 'They're not quite ripe yet, but when they're still hard, they have all their flavour.'

We said goodbye to Paco. He stood watching his water-courses as they made their complicated strands downwards from the secret spring and past his feet. He was leaning on his hoe handle. I could do that, I thought; I'd like to do that.

Susan and I followed Pilar up through the contours of their land.

'We have almonds and walnuts,' she said. 'And look – there's our new onions.'

'They're swelling up fine,' I said.

'Pick one. Take two.'

I pulled one, and shook off the loose earth. It was a young onion, but already big. Its stem was that of a decent leek. 'Thanks very much,' I said. I was still uncertain, absurdly, about whether or not our carrier-bags full of unexpected bounty were to be paid for. Pilar picked some apricots and topped up the small room remaining atop my oranges and lemons and the onion. The handle, under the great weight, had become thin as a cheese-wire to bite into the joints of my fingers.

By a meandering path, we worked our way back up to the gap in the wall; we admired their nut trees and their vines, a patch of peppers and tomatoes; and then we sauntered, chatting all the way, back to the shop. I felt I should buy a few items: sardines, biscuits, a sausage – not that I needed them.

'There's the fruit,' I said. 'What do I owe you for all this lovely fruit?'

'*Nada*,' she said. 'Nothing.'

'You are incredibly generous, Pilar.'

She cackled in that way of hers, and waved me away.

Heavily laden, we got into the car and shook our heads in wonderment. And, as we drove down the mountain road back to Cerros del Lago, I wished I'd thought to ask how much the rental would be for the house that contained machines.

After the morning in the orchard, I began to feel as though I could be happy again, given time. I had been able once more to exult in the beauty of the world and the unreflecting goodness of some of the creatures in it. I drank little that night, feeling less in need of the bottle's promise of oblivion; I knew myself more naturally relaxed than I had felt for years. I was almost blithe: almost, I say, because I could not help but sense that it might be ignoble of me to admit, yet, to the possibility of sporadic absences of sorrow in what remained of life. Wasn't it a callous act of treachery towards my dead wife to suppose that I could find a way of doing without her? It was an unanswerable poser; but when I went to bed, I tried not to make the usual tense, tight fists of my hands or crunch myself into a ball to try to keep my terrors out. Nor did I have the recurring nightmare in which I had no option but to stand on the precarious edge of a vast, dry tank acrawl with hideous reptiles and land-fish snapping at me with elongated, serrated jaws. I had glimpsed a version of paradise, one I might some time have a share of, and I did my best to bury my guilt for having indulged in this premature, voyeuristic peeping.

However, I received an immediate come-uppance. The following morning, I awoke to find my body almost entirely smothered in scarlet blotches, weals, cross-hatched corrugations and stipplings. Also, my lips were hugely swollen, like a porpoise's lips; I found I could scarcely speak through them coherently: the only consonant I could make with my sudden blubber was an overwhelming 'm'. In the bathroom I inspected myself all over. My skin was that of a high-complexioned waxwork figure beginning to pucker and melt. Below my navel was an area that gave the nubbled effect of my having spent the night, belly-down, in a cauldron-size colander. Properly scared, not knowing what to do for the best, I put on some clothes, wrapped a towel round my head so as not to alarm my daughter with the most startling of my several disfigurements; then went to her room to tell her what had happened and to ask her what she thought I might do about it.

'Mah-mah-mah,' I said.

'Morning, Old Bean,' she said. 'Auditioning for the Invisible Man?'

It's not a straightforward business, with limited vocables, to make lucid communication through swathes of terry-cloth. I did my best. Susan was not unsympathetic: which is to say that, when I unwrapped the towel to reveal the monstrous oedema of my maw, she tried very hard not to laugh, which made me laugh. For she had made light of my trivial if dramatic affliction, the way good daughters correctly do with fathers prone to hypochondria. This helped to de-fuse my fright and dispel self-pity. Performing through my preposterous lips, I rendered four bars of an impersonation of Al Jolson singing 'Mammy', the one song apt for my ring-doughnut mouthings. Then, 'Mhat moo minky mis?' I asked her.

'Nettle-rash, acute form of,' she said. 'You probably got some kind of pollen or flying seeds in your clothes yesterday.'

'Mah. Mon't minker mam me memmle-mash.'

'Your lips could be from mosquito bites in the night.'

'Mah.'

'Maybe an allergy. Something you've eaten. A food additive – like the red colouring they put in *chorizo*.'

'Mha' man ah moo, mem?'

'Go down to the chemist's in San Pedro. Show the man. He'll know what to give you – antihistamine, or whatever. Then I thought we could go to Cordova or somewhere for a day or two. Change of scene do you good. Me too.'

Once we were beyond Ronda, my eruptions and efflorescences began to subside. My lips, too, like blow-up bladders with slow punctures, gradually deflated.

Not until another eighteen months had passed was I to realise what had happened to me. I was much debilitated; the body had to excrete, one way or another, the accumulated stress of several years. Some mourners, I was to discover, are prey to nervous breakdowns, ulcers, and much, much worse: chronic arthritic conditions, heart attacks, even cancer. Some collapse in what has been described as 'a kind of psychic giving up'. This is probably what accounts for so many instances, in centuries gone by, of persons dying of grief or 'a broken heart', a condition not recognised as such by the medical profession. My comparatively minor – though distressing – symptoms were to recur many times: not always so dramatically, and usually following an attack of guilt and self-recrimination. It ought to be routine for newly bereaved people to be warned of the physical manifestations of a violently changed psychological state. Lorna and I had the same group of GPs; I could have been forewarned by one of them about the possible effects of her death on my health. My guess is (though I have no evidence to put forward for this) that new widows and widowers used to be given commonsensical advice by their doctor, soon after the funeral. Old Campbell-Petters, whose house I had bought two decades before, would surely have beckoned to me from his dispensary window and called me in for a whisky-and-water and a ten-minute, caring chat. Nowadays, group practice waiting-room notice-boards are a blizzard of leaflets advertising whatever is trendiest in welfare concern: diet fads, weight-watching, 'well-woman' clinics, cervical smears, toddler groups and such; but the eternal problem of what to do about being bereft of one's life partner is ignored. I was to become obsessed with the notion that my periodic rashes were due to the 'E-number' contents of foods I had not carefully checked before consuming them. I read the small print on labels of cans and packets, eschewed caramel and tartrazine and stuffs known only by their complicated chemical equations. I could have done with some rough-hewn wisdom passed on to me by a family patriarch who had gone through a similar experience to my own, and who knew the essential steps of survival as surely as he knew when the weather was right for sowing runner beans.

By late afternoon we had reached the small city of Écija (resignedly nick-named 'The Frying-pan' by its citizens) which habitually records the highest summer temperatures in western Europe. We were fortunate to find rooms, having arrived on the eve of the departure of the local contingent on their annual trek to the shrine of El Rocío. From upper windows of the *hostal* I saw returning exiles bringing forth from the boots of their cars their *fiesta* garb: the men their Cordoban hats and leather waistcoats and cowboy chaps and high-heeled boots; the women their layered dresses in vivid greens and reds and yellows and blue-and-white polka-dots, and their fancy shawls and tortoiseshell combs and oversized artificial carnations for their hair.

The scene next morning in the main square and in the smaller adjacent square outside the cathedral, was a wonderful conglomeration of jubilant colours. Freshly painted and flower-decorated carts, with canvas covers stretched over iron hoops, were neatly parked behind their patient, snuffling pairs of horses. Other, more splendid horses of pure Arab stock, immaculately groomed and furnished with gleaming and luxuriant saddles and bridles, stood in an orderly line facing a white arcade; their male riders waited, chain-smoking, for their wives (some of whom were to sit side-saddle behind them in their finery) to emerge from Mass. At the very gate of the cathedral, backed up as close as possible to its handsome ironwork, was the entirely white-and-silver cart which was to lead the Écija procession on its pilgrimage. Harnessed to it were two oxen, caparisoned with neck-bands and belly-bands in the Spanish national colours of yellow and red, waiting for the city's Madonna to be brought outside; the beasts had numbers branded into their flanks, and their neck-bands were strung with a peal of miniature bells to jingle through their long journey. A tiny man, wielding a staff half again as tall as himself, tended the beasts, tapping their hocks ever so gently to keep them in line, orderly as a ceremonial guard of honour.

Inside, they were in the middle of the Gloria. I had never before witnessed such an idiosyncratic celebration of the *agape*. The bishop, attendant priests, acolytes and servers, wore traditional vestments: but the choir, band, packed congregation –

predominantly, as usual, women and children – were mostly garbed in traditional local costume; and, moreover, playing and singing an indigenous, *flamenco*, version of the Mass. The music was made with guitars, mandolins and castanets. The singers sang the full-throated, weird, half-Arabic chord patterns I had often heard before – though authentically only in low, bull-fighting bars or emanating from mysterious, slatternly yards of the poorer quarters of out-of-the-way small towns, well off the tourist routes. I stood by the font, my heart bursting with the excitement of hearing those magnificent new (for me) settings of Credo, Sanctus and Benedictus. I was entranced by exuberant panoplies of lovely women, the sopranos and altos who rose and sat and sometimes danced with sinuous arms aloft. It was a properly vernacular rite they sang, in an idiom that had belonged to them and their people for as long as memory could tell; evangelical and popular in tone, yet somehow possessing its own formality, too. It was fervent yet correct, honest, reverent, deeply imbued with an unself-conscious integrity. The English counterparts of these people (and I visualised them) had lost track of their inheritance in this matter, as in so many others.

In the main square a kind of beadle, who carried an elaborately-worked silver wand of office, was lining up carts, carriages, horsemen and hikers: tall, slender *hidalgos* (the cousins of Sloane Rangers), stubby little peasant farmers in broad red braces with their wobbling old wives; fair women in the prime of life with their several daughters, all in different-coloured dresses, holding hands in a line the width of the street. When they moved off at the comfortable pace set by the oxen, the stay-at-home bystanders in workaday clothes applauded them on their way. The square emptied; and only now did one notice how elegant its buildings were, how expertly sculptured were its round citrus trees, how graceful its palms.

In Cordova, though it was the last day of a week's fiesta, the city was still thrumming with energy and whole-hearted fun. Along the broad, central avenue, splendid young men paraded on high-stepping, mettlesome stallions. They did this to show

74

off their equestrian skills and the beauty of their ladies, riding pillion; also – and not least – their own good looks and panache. If their partners should dismount, they challenged each other to furious races, galloping a clattering kilometre along hot asphalt, and then – presumably to allow some repose to their public vanity – loitering awhile in groups of their peers, testing out their braggadocio on each other, as their superb animals gratefully drank at the trough, or pawed, restless, at the kerb.

Parallel with the avenue, and running the length of both sides of it, were wide strips of continuous parkland: grass and sandy rides, with enough mature trees to give shade without getting in the way of plenty of unrestrained activity. These strips were divided into dozens of spaces roughly the area of, say, half a junior football pitch, each one the temporary, *al fresco*, H.Q. of some local club or society. Entry was open and free to all comers; and it was the custom to flit from one to another, enjoying a beer in this one, a snack in another, a bout of conversation and bonhomie in the next. There would be, typically, a long bar set up on trestles along one side, continuously busy serving food as well as drinks, a small stage, and, between the two, well-spaced café tables with iron chairs, all of which you could move for the convenience of your group without having some busybody raising objections. The atmosphere was that of an easy-going night-club that had neglected to close during daylight hours. We sampled some on one side of the avenue; ate prawns and stewed peppers, saw off a glass or two of *fino*; and I secretly lusted after a magnificent lady, my age, and only slightly too Junoesque for her red layered dress, who danced on a bare stage – solo, rapt – as lubriciously erotic an interpretation of the *sevillana* as I ever hope to witness.

Then we crossed the avenue to visit an enclosure crammed with people sitting at a table-arrangement which recalled occasions in England such as annual cricket club dinners or Rotary lunches. I asked at the gate whether we might come in, as it seemed as if it might be a specially private function, but we were welcomed as warmly as if we had been old friends. What had evidently been a long meal was drawing to a close; table-cloths bore the evidence of the wreckage of dessert. We sat down, and were given wine. The company was jolly, loud, and sporting paper hats. Most, I then noticed, were mentally disabled: Down's syndrome persons, and others of sub-normal intelligence. All looked rapturously happy. At the top table, one of the helpers (or, as we would have to say in England, 'carers') made a short speech of thanks to the cooks. And then the small lady next to her, after some conventional joshing, chaff, banter and good-natured chai-aiking, stood up and sang for us.

She could not have been described as a victim of the syndrome that had entrapped her since conception. She wore bright fiesta clothes, her hair had been coiffed in the Andalusian manner, and she took an entirely confident place in society: to all appearances not one to be gawped at or embarrassedly avoided by passers-by as would happen in England. How old she was, I could not say: but of course she would not live long. She sang in the pure tones of a little girl's voice; a folk song, with a chorus after every verse for the company to join in. When she had finished, she received her applause like a *diva*. My much-battered old straw hat, which had been going the rounds of the tables, found its way on to the top of her head; and they clapped her again. When we left, another song was beginning. Someone else was the special performer, a hero, a heroine, a precious brother or sister, son or daughter, whose life was no less important than anybody else's, and not only capable of being fulfilled with the love of relatives and friends, but mutely, clamorously, gloriously, demanding it. The plaintive little song I'd heard was to stay in my head for days: an inspiration to embrace life again, and to keep on embracing it.

I said I'd like to go to the bullfight. 'Do you mind?' I said to Susan. 'You don't have to come.'

'Oh, but I think I'd like to.'

'Doubt whether you'll enjoy it. And nobody's allowed to approve of it. I don't, any more.'

'So why do you go?'

I had been an *aficionado* since my teens. I knew all the arguments by heart. I explained, but could not justify, my ambivalent attitude. Were I dictator of Spain, I'd ban the barbarity; while it's still legal, I'll buy the best seat I can afford. We studied a garish poster slapped up on a garage door.

'What's *rejoneo*?'

'Bullfighting from horseback. Not the nasty, pig-sticking stuff picadors do in ordinary corridas. Wonderful, elegant horsemanship. The kind of control that makes all that Earls Court stuff look like donkey rides at the beach.'

. Susan had once had every little girl's fascination with horses. During the afternoon, she had been daring herself to ask for a canter on one of the flashy young men's stallions.

'Let's be moral lepers,' she said; and she stumped up the price of her ticket.

When we had taken our seats and the tinny band had struck up a lively *paso doble*, I said, 'Your mum loved all this, you know. I never thought she would, but she did. The first bullfight I took her to was in Salamanca, a couple of years after my summer away in Cuenca.'

I could remember precisely how she looked, sitting beside me in the full sunlight of late afternoon. We had been lucky to get tickets. I had bought her a new dress for the occasion; white, with a few small scarlet buttons to replace the original pearl ones, and trimmings she made herself from a length of ribbon. I never saw her look more lovely – not even as a young woman, not even as the girl I had met when she was sixteen. That bullfight had been an excellent one: good bulls artistically fought, competently and cleanly killed. I told Lorna how lucky she had been: usually, only two or three of the six bulls could be expected to provide such a thrilling and aesthetically satisfying spectacle. She was avid for an expert's knowledge of the ceremonies, the different types of pass with the cape. Afterwards, as we walked back towards the city centre, I was as proud as any *señorito* with his new girl.

Now, in Cordova, I found myself involuntarily doing and saying things I had done and said in Salamanca. It was eerie, like being part of a cleverly devised illusion. I bought cans of iced beer. I pointed out the President's box and the gate of the *toril*. I told Susan what to look out for in the opening ceremony.

'So beautiful. Unforgettable,' I said; and the words upset me.

One of the *rejoneadores* was a Portuguese. He wore a pink satin frock-coat of eighteenth-century cut, a tricorn hat, and the sort of breeches you see in paintings by Gainsborough. The Spaniards were in the grey-and-black rancher's gear we had been seeing all through the afternoon, wherever *sevillanas* were being performed. Now we saw a dance perhaps even more memorable: an equine, taurine ballet of twists and turns, slower or faster gyrations, approachings and retreatings, the participants as though connected by invisible elastic. When the first rider had planted his rosettes – languidly, nonchalant – it was time for him to dismount and kill. He took his cape and sword.

'I'll tell you when it's time to turn away,' I said. And I thought, that's nice: a perfect iambic pentameter out of nowhere, complete with a helpful internal alliteration. I wrote it down on my programme while the business was being done on the sand. Not that anything would come of the words. The gift was gone. Sometimes a remnant of it would torment me, as now, with a handy *donnée*; and it would make me feel, for a little while, the way I had always used to when a poem surprisingly announced itself. Then the words would go immediately stale, like bits of a loaf broken open and left in the sun. But these words surely, would generate something powerful? *I'll tell you when it's time to turn away*. They were the gist of what Lorna had said when, home again and in our bedroom after her first big operation, she had to remove the obdurator and perform the complex cleansing of her mouth. Here I was, saying to my daughter what her mother had said to me: which was what I had said to her mother on an earlier occasion, also at a bullfight, before so much unpleasantness had begun. How could I knit those components together: the circumstances, the two women, the diverse excitements, the pity, the colour, the sudden passions, the being in the presence of a death to be imminently observed? No, nothing would come of my poem.

I was afraid of it. It was already stillborn, the evanescence of itself. Somehow, I'd lost the courage as well as the knack. You need a strong stomach for poetry.

The bull was dragged out. Five more were dealt with, and we left. Maybe I would never go to another *corrida*, I thought. I was glad when night fell and the lights came on throughout the city. We shared a comically large paper cone full of *churros*, visited bars so noisy that the shouted syllables seemed to shatter like glass and prick and tingle on your skin. For five days and nights the fiesta had been going on. Still it continued, with an energy that showed no sign of exhausting itself. Happy groups of friends sang and chattered through the streets; families, from great-grandparents to babes-in-arms, gathered in force to cram the avenue's enclosures, all talking at once, like delirious parrots, round high piles of seafood, salads, chipped roundels of fresh bread; fire-crackers detonated, near and far; balloons, trailing their strings, were caught in the lower branches of trees, or sailed up and away into the night; impromptu stalls sold coconut ice and *turrón* and nutty confections without a name. There were bits of funfair which had been invisible in the daylight, but which now came out into the full bloom of their patterned lights, like vast, nocturnal flowers; and everywhere there was music: you moved from one set of sounds into another, live guitar to 'top ten' cassettes, from marches to rock, experiencing an effect at once unnerving, disorienting and stimulating, like that produced by a Charles Ives symphony.

When it had gone one o'clock, we went back to the car. Needing directions to the hotel we'd selected at the edge of the town, I stopped by a group of policemen slap in the middle of an intersection. They were laughing, as full of carnival spirit as the crowds of masqueraders they held up the traffic for.

'Could you please help me find my way –'

'Yes, *caballero*. Where are you from?'

'England.'

'Madrid, Paris. Keep going – you can't miss it! Ha-Ha!'

'Ha-ha-ha!'

Constabulary humour is universal; but what happened next

does not occur in my part of England. After I'd given the name of the hotel, the policeman said, 'Follow us.' He and one of his partners ran to their nearby car, switched on its flashing light and scorched away, scattering the throng as a power-boat throws aside the spume from its bow-wave.

Late as it was, and though the fiesta was at last collapsing like a long-blazing bonfire becoming its ashes, the hotel gladly provided us with a meal. The waiter, between courses, stared wistfully out of the window at the revellers going home. It was already Monday morning, a new week of work was beginning; but he, like his fellow-citizens, had enjoyed his fiesta. Already he was looking forward to the next one.

'This wasn't the main fiesta, you understand. Oh, no. For that, you must come back later in the summer! In your country, you have fiestas, no?'

Oh dear no, I thought. There's a period in high summer when Chichester had its 'Festival': high-falutin shennanigins for the respectable cognoscenti at the theatre and in the cathedral and various smaller venues – redundant churches, mainly; muddy pots and muddier pictures at exhibitions by worthy amateurs, the odd outré happening or stunt promoted by students, seemingly out of sheer boredom; recitals in the Bishop's Palace kitchen, given by faded local playwrights and poets (me included) to audiences redolent of lavender and talc; a season of plays, playing safe with, typically, a sure-fire Shakespeare, a Restoration dud taken down and given a dusting, and, perhaps, if we're lucky, Sir Peter Ustinov's latest offering. No diversion but what had been sanctioned by the 'good taste' of the Rotary, the Chamber of Commerce, the Townswomen's Guild, the twinset-and-pearls and pinstripe brigade of philistine cliques. The people's festival, such as it was, occurred during a few hours of a Saturday; and a glum business it was, too: a dispiriting procession of 'floats' mounted on lorries, the often unenthusiastic-looking participants in unambitious, uninventive costumes; here and there a dire, and as though press-ganged, band; lines of old bunting, their colours all but rinsed away; and, bringing up the rear, a number of trade vehicles, their only contribution to jollity being the advertisement of their sponsoring firms: the schools of motoring, the double-glazers, the coal merchants, the building societies. All this to the accompaniment and ceaseless importunities of persons clanking coins in buckets: for in a town like Chichester, even this version of public enjoyment could only be justified if done in the name of a Good Cause. You could look for spontaneity and exuberance, for the generation of gaiety and the provision of fun, but you would look all but in vain for it in the tiring traipse of the Carnival. At the real ale and jazz festival in one of the parks you might find traces of good cheer; but only in the two hundred minutes after the music started (late) and before the licensing time expired (early). In the streets, what amenities? Where could you sit? What was there to watch? What was there to eat and drink? Where were the stalls, the street-vendors, the throwers of streamers, the masks, the fancy dresses, the fireworks? Where were the banners and the fairy-lights and flags? A few years back, an old-established ironmonger's (now, alas, defunct) courted prosecution (on the grounds of 'unfair trading') for displaying a single, diminutive Union Jack from an upper window. Letters of complaint appeared in the newspaper. The offending object was removed. Subsequently, the City Fathers ordained that a small number of what they (in all seriousness and solemnity) termed 'Celebration Brackets' should be affixed to certain, approved, strategically spaced façades; and so it was that, on certain, approved, strategically spaced occasions, these very brackets, duly furnished with poles, were permitted to bear approved flags.

'Yes,' I said to the waiter. 'We have our festivals, too.'

'Ours are nothing like the old days.'

'We shan't need pudding,' I said. 'Did you go to the bull-fight?'

'Bah! Bulls like lap-dogs. Horses like camels, *Nada!*'

We talked about our day. I had been unreflectingly happy. Then Susan said, apropos the bulls, 'Did Mum mind about the blood?'

FIVE

O F COURSE she must have minded the recurrent appearance of blood; but squeamishness was not her way. She
kept her distress to herself, concealed any red-soiled tissues as
best she could. But she could not hide certain acute moments of
pathos. Ever since I had known her, after brushing her hair and
completing her make-up, she had had a habit of taking a final
look at herself in the mirror, making the sort of face naughty
children pull behind the backs of adults, then sticking out her
tongue. She never did that now. After using the Higg's
apparatus (a length of fearsome orange tubing with a bulb,
with which to rinse the new interstice in her jaw) she would
replace the cleansed prosthesis, tidy away her comb and cosmetics, then simply contemplate her lop-sided image for a few
seconds, to all appearances impassively. She made gruesome
jokes against herself whenever there was some fresh development she could not keep from me. 'I'm wearing out and falling
apart,' she would say, the way she had used to when she needed
new glasses or a visit to the chiropodist; events had turned the
joke black, but she expected me to laugh with her – however
mirthlessly – when so prompted. Indeed, as the illness progressed, it was as though she had discovered in herself a seam of
humour which she had long kept buried – perhaps from
shyness, perhaps because she thought wit was my preserve, as
needlework was hers. She became sharper, quicker on the
uptake, at times very funny indeed; more inclined to offer
opinions, to disagree, to debate issues. We took to doing *The*

Times crossword puzzle together; and, through this, I became aware that she had a much wider range of general knowledge than I had previously supposed; and so, as had happened very often before, I rediscovered her, loved her the more for having become, in part, someone new to me.

We made visits, twice a week, to the M.F.U. clinic. I became thoroughly familiarised with each of the two consulting rooms. I knew how to operate the super-complicated dentist's chairs; and I knew, precisely, the contents of every cupboard and drawer; where this implement belonged, where that dressing would be found. She was routinely inspected by the consultant surgeon, the registrar, various housemen and an ever-changing platoon of students; she was attended to by staff nurses. The permanent obdurator, which had been fashioned and fitted by two kindly technicians in an adjoining workshop, was minutely adjusted week by week. Everyone, including the Red Cross volunteer receptionist and the clerk, called her by her first name. By dint of her patience, her endurance and her uncomplaining nature, she became what is known as a 'character'. The file containing her medical history now ran to two fat volumes. We dutifully obeyed instructions to go to X-ray, to Path. Lab., to Pharmacy. She submitted herself to being the subject, or object, of teaching seminars. Often we were obliged to hang about for long periods – in the corridor, if the waiting area was full. If we finished the crossword puzzle, or were stumped by it and conversation flagged, I would sometimes have a harrowing glimpse of other patients being called to the consulting room: one woman, most grotesquely, with a head which had been left elongated, like a cobra-head; another, a man whose mouth was crammed with what looked like a rat-trap. Shuddering, I would announce that I'd go and fetch cups of coffee for us. Lorna had to remain in case she were called; so, cravenly, I would desert her instead of diverting her, and I spent stolen, liberated minutes at the WVS refreshment stall, steadying my panic as I queued, in the contemplation of hissing urns and stacks of chocolate bars.

At home, she surprised me one day. 'Guess what I can do?'

she said; and she produced a stick of celery and took a man-sized bite and crunched it. I had been concocting a mess of mincemeat and vegetables in the blender. For joy, I would have thrown it down the sink. 'No – don't waste it,' she said. A point of honour, it was with her, not to celebrate a milestone on the road to recovery we had made a pretence of assuming she would reach. What she did do, though, was to start work on a new embroidery. She set up her frame, tacked canvas on it and, after painstakingly working out her design on squared paper, began an illuminated version of the Prayer of St Richard. The text, checked from the printed card I had brought from the cathedral, was to be decorated with vines and spring flowers. Though she never said as much, I knew this was to be her votive offering of thanks for having survived. By now she had resumed many of her routine chores of housework; she could drive, look after her parents, do a little gardening. And, as confidence grew, she felt able to spend some time away from home; indeed, further away from the M.F.U. than would be comfortable, should an emergency occur. One of the wickedest things I have ever done in my life was to lose my temper with her, over some trivial thing, in an hotel we stayed at in Wales over one weekend. I made her cry, and I had meant to. It was an awful, convulsive sobbing and helpless wailing such as I'd never once seen her do. I had got used, without realising it, to her seeming to be better; the Tupperware box containing the boracic powder and the swabs and tweezers and Higg's apparatus had become a familiar, ordinary, no longer threatening item on the bathroom shelf. I had entered the illusion she had created for me. Her terrible tears, as she lay on the bed with her back to me, broke that illusion. To this day I feel the useless remorse with which I stroked her hair, knowing again how threads of her tumour were still on the move in her, centimetres under my fingertips.

It goes without saying that I would sooner not have made Lorna cry so piteously; but I can't be sorry that, for a few minutes, a sense of the possibility of the continuance of life, however rudely it barged in, illuminated the quotidian gloom of existing forever under threat. Would it have been better, in those unguarded instants, if I'd alluded to dreams for our distant future, to prospects of some far-off joy? Probably not. The inevitable jolt back to the reality of her predicament would have resulted in tears even more bitter than those occasioned by my hurtfulness. Just a few short interims of being carefree for the enjoyment of the unremarkable pleasures of the moment: those would have been a balm for her, and for me. I was to hate myself for making her cry over a trifle. I wish I had been able to make her cry, instead, again and again, earlier during our marriage, with the spectacle of a landscape or a poignant sentence or two, or a newly-discovered melody. And I wish I could have made her laugh until she ached. About anything. But I never loved her any the less because I hadn't been able to. Liked her less, sometimes, maybe: but love doesn't work like that.

When she had done with her crying, and she turned to face me, I hoped, forlornly, that she would, just for once, scream and slap my face in retaliation for my verbal brutality – the way, just once, and many years before, she had thrown a saucepan at me, rarely and most endearingly enraged. But what she did was to say she understood the stress I was under. I apologised. We embraced, and that was that: for this was our *modus vivendi*.

★

Poor old England, too, had long been corroding from within. Her good looks – in city and town, village and open country – were fading; she was an exhausted country, 'wearing out, falling apart', the very last of her energy draining away; too spent to protest, she had got used to putting up with second best and third rate; was endlessly uncomplaining; able and willing to endure her malaise, she was therefore worthy of a kind of admiration and respectful pity – though pity is an ignominious emotion. She clung resignedly to a few features of former glory: once lovely mementos kept, from a sense of dread sentimentality, in a mothballed drawer, lustreless and gathering dust. It was in fierce despair that I loved my poor motherland.

I do mean England. Scotland, Wales and Northern Ireland are foreign countries to me. I do not know what to make of 'Britain' or 'Great Britain' or 'The British Isles' – and least of all 'The UK' which is a concept spoken about, in my experience, only by such as Customs and Immigration officials, and disaffected, yet paradoxically super-patriotic, expatriates.

Susan and I spent a day in Gibraltar. There is no better place for seeing the worst aspects of contemporary England: for candid Spanish sunlight entirely illuminates all upon which it falls.

It was hard for us to find anything to admire as we progressed up Main Street. This, throughout its rising and twisting length, was a kind of monumental visual aid for demonstrating every symptom of a deeply cynical, materialistic society knowing the price of everything and the value of nothing. Where, here, could one spend cash not just on objects to plug in but on the quality of life? The answer, we told ourselves, was probably on a taxi-ride back to the frontier post. Any self-respecting and dignified people would have long since demanded honest independence, else acquiesced in a restoration of Spanish authority. Gibraltar was the culture of the airport duty-free area writ large, every other business dealing in tax-reduced liquor and scent. The shop-keepers were sly, ravenous for money. The worst features of an English High Street were all to be found here, much magnified: gross overcrowding of people and traffic (the car being a ludicrous totem, having nowhere to go and nowhere to be still); preponderance of consumer durable goods – overwhelmingly, of electrical, electronic and optical devices of oriental provenance and manufacture – over comestibles; awful, parody 'pubs'; infrequent cafés – squalid, over-priced, complete with the surly service of appalling food; souvenir boutiques, each one a jubilee of whatever was trumpery, tawdry, naff. I looked for something hilariously horrible to buy as a souvenir, but had to give up, confronted by an embarrassment of impoverishments too teeming to choose from.

'Let's go home,' I said to Susan. By 'home' I meant not England but the Spanish apartment where, perhaps not so temporarily, I was hanging my hat. She, on the other hand, had no option but to catch her flight back to London. I was to be on my own again.

★

And, to make matters worse, possibly incommunicado as far as mail was concerned

One afternoon, the younger Warboys girl came to the door. She looked troubled. I asked her in. As was the custom, she removed her shoes before entering.

'Mum's very upset.'

'Oh, dear. What's up?'

'She's just had a letter from Sally. Mum isn't very pleased that you told her about ... you know.'

'No – I don't know.'

'About my uncle being in here when you arrived.'

'But I didn't tell Sally that!'

'Well, she's found out somehow. And she's really told Mum off about it.'

'Oh, Lord.'

'So I don't know what's going to happen about your post from now on.'

My mail was still being sent care of Vicky Warboys at her school in San Pedro. One or other of the girls would obligingly leave it under a brick on my balcony.

'I think I know what's happened. I probably told my brother about the mix-up when I wrote to him. Making a joke of it, I mean. Daresay he mentioned it to Sally, not dreaming it'd cause any trouble. Look – I would never have told tales out of school, now would I? Will you tell your Mum that for me? Tell her I'm very sorry if I've been the cause of embarrassment. But I didn't do it on purpose – honest.'

87

It was hard on the girl, being a go-between.

'Listen,' I said, 'shall I come and talk to your Mum?'

'I don't think you'd better. This came for you today.' She handed me a buff envelope. 'But from now on, I don't know.' And she went out on to the balcony, slipped on her shoes and ran up the steps to the street.

I was in a fix. At the time, I had all kinds of business to attend to: the proofs of my *Selected Poems*, correspondence with the bank, building societies, the Rating Department, the Water Company and, as I now saw glumly, from the Inland Revenue. More important, though, was my personal post. I relied on letters from family and friends to keep my spirits up and, so to speak, to keep my disintegrating identity from falling into bad repair. There was nothing for it but to make a few phone calls and arrange for my mail to be addressed henceforward to Cerros del Lago, taking a chance on the sporadic postal service. Items already in transit, I hoped, would with luck survive the present seething ill-will of Vicky Warboys. I spent an hour with a bottle of wine, re-reading every one of the letters I had so far received from home, and sorting them. Each pile made up a testimony of love or affection different from all the others; each writer had his or her own way of being supportive: the loving, the jaunty, the chatty, the anecdotal, the allusive, the direct, the wise, the commonsensical, the fey. One of them, in particular, was able to write with utter perspicacity about grief. This was Lorna's best friend, Audrey.

She was well qualified to do so. She had seen her husband, John, die of a heart attack only three months before Lorna. Five days before Lorna, her father died. The letters we exchanged had little in the way of comfort or solace to offer: what they did was to share the experience we had in common, and thus help us both towards an understanding of the bleakness for which there can be no adequate preparation; thus, they took the worst of the chill off desolation. Up till the moment when her father's illness took her up to Lincolnshire, Audrey had been a frequent visitor at Lorna's hospital bedside; within a few days of attending one funeral, she returned to Sussex to attend another.

We had gravitated towards each other as bits of flotsam will. Now she was in the West Riding of Yorkshire, helping friends run a bed-and-breakfast establishment in a remote farmhouse. She occupied a room scarcely bigger than a cupboard, but this, with the constant company of her friends and guests, was much better than having the sole occupancy of an entire house. We had both fled from home: she north, I south. In my letters I would describe sundrenched, deserted mountainsides dotted with isolated pomegranate trees; in hers, she told of rain-drenched moors where not even a solitary horse could be seen against the skyline. Our sub-texts spoke plangently clear from the local colour of the images we picked: that is, of our several emptinesses.

The four of us had been friends for twenty years. Having moved to the area at much the same time, we met through taking part in the village pantomime, which was produced by the headmistress of the school our children attended. Ever since, we had seen each other more or less regularly, first at parties, then over dinners at their house or ours, robust meals which were usually followed by games of Mah Jong, Monopoly and such. We all spent a Christmas together one year when I was unaccountably flush. Lorna and I had recently bought our annexe from Dr Campbell-Petters, after his retirement. In the waiting-room of the former surgery we set up all the tables we could find for a sumptuous, Victorian-style family feast for nineteen people. I contributed a game pie about a yard square, all glistering under the glaze of egg-yolk I'd lavished it with like a *vernissage*.

We had in common our chronic hard-upness, apart from the joys and tribulations of raising children. And when the Mah Jong tiles had been put back in their box, we might discuss plans – usually implausible or downright fanciful – for making cash to finance schemes for a putative future where none of our careers was ever likely to lead us. But – after our respective families had grown up – what enterprises and what travels we embarked upon in those kitchen chairs!

As a result of these often fantastical speculations, I grew very fond of John. Though we never became intimate friends, the pals that Lorna and Audrey were, we were closer than mere acquaintances, always glad to see each other and able, when we did so, to pick up from where we had left off before. An architect, he had had youthful aspirations to be a writer; a writer, I had always hankered after practical skills such as his. We were both dreamers after our own fashion. He was much given to sudden, chirpy bursts of infectious, acclamatory laughter. These always seemed to me like an occasional brief release from a self-imposed sentence of imprisoning anxiety: for John was an inveterate worrier; life was a rough terrain for him to cross. He was cursed with an equable temperament, incapable of violence, spite or malice. He would not lash out, shout and storm, puncture the film of his inner bubble of frustration to allow his rage to disperse. Instead, he let his stresses secrete and gather. His funeral took place on my birthday. Lorna, with four months and two days of her life left, was present. I was honoured and touched to be asked to speak his eulogy; and though the words were not, and could not have been, adequate, I spoke them as best I could in the village church before we followed his coffin outside to his grave by the beech hedge in its brown winter leaves.

I had given Susan a letter to post to Audrey after she landed at Heathrow. In it, I had struck a more cheerful note than usual, describing a talkative old man who had come to scythe the scrubby grass of the slope beneath my balcony. Later in the year, he'd told me, he would be back, bringing a long pole with which to knock down the carobs to feed his master's horses. Susan's visit had enlivened me, I'd said, and now I was looking forward to the arrival of my elder son, Ed, and his girlfriend, Sheila. Meanwhile I was alone with unavoidable thoughts of the recent past. Anything I saw might prompt them.

Whenever I caught sight of one of those large butane storage tanks installed outside a house, I recalled Lorna's description of the body scanner she had to enter when the trouble had turned worse again: like an elongated bathysphere. I had waited outside the Midhurst hospital, walking the trim grounds. I knew the interior, having once written an article about it for a local paper; it was beautifully constructed, not like most of the hospitals we knew, with heavy, hard-wood doors and expensive fittings. 'Don't tell me any more,' I said to her. 'Let's have a cream tea on the way home. You'd like that.' The very notion of having to submit to such a claustrophobic examination filled me with terror. I imagined – though it was probably nothing like this at all – a great wheel having been turned to clamp her in, tight shut, like that on a bank vault or the hatch of a submarine – while, possibly in total darkness, the rays made their inroads through every tissue and fibre of her body, exploring, seeking out the bad in a whirring ministry. After the plates had revealed their evidence, the following week we had to go to yet another hospital new to us, in Guildford, where she was examined by her own consultant and at least half a dozen others. They were grave, and they muttered in a huddle. They were unanimous: she must lose her right eye.

Words are my trade. I graduated as a linguist. I have taught myself the disciplines of verse and prose and the drama. But there was nothing I knew how to say at that moment.

We got in the car.

Lorna said, 'I wonder whether I'll still be able to drive?'

'You learned how to bite a stick of celery.'

She closed her right eye and practised seeing only with her left.

'You have to turn your head more,' she said.

'Maybe you'll have to pass your driving test again.'

I accelerated for home, where we could properly attend to our distress. Soon she'll only be able to shed half the tears, I was thinking. We got home. We got through another week. We packed her case: the night-clothes, the drugs, the toilet-bag, the Tupperware box of tricks, the clown. I almost said, 'Don't forget to take something to read.' But then I saw she'd already packed two detective novels; also a small album of family photographs.

She went through the familiar routine of admission, took up

her station at what was now her usual bed, arranged her things. The locker was on her right side; she would have to turn her head right round to see the laughing clown next day. I stayed as long as I could bear to; then I went, but only as far as the car-park. I stood by the car, squeezing the keys in my palm and cursing myself for my spineless dereliction; and then, after a short while, I went back and stayed until they made me go. Taking leave of each other earlier had been an agony. This second time was worse. By the lift I held her in my arms but not so close that I could not look into her eyes. She knew what I was doing, and she looked back at me intensely, trying not to blink. I kissed her on each closed lid, the way I had used to as a boy, in the first amazement of my prize. When her eyes were open again, I took yet another last look. I had always loved the particular blue of them, the blue of Chalk Hill butterflies.

At the hour next morning when I knew the operation was about to take place, I went not to the cathedral but to the village church. I found it locked. I rattled the latch. Aghast, I drove hard for the next village. Half-way there, I saw the assistant priest cycling towards me. I sounded my horn, braked hard, got out and slammed the door. I ran across the road and grabbed his elbow. I was scarcely able to speak.

'St George's is locked, for heaven's sake.'

'We have to keep it locked. Vandals, you know.'

'But what am I to do?' I told him what was happening. He was a thoroughly good and pleasant man, with a saintly face dominated by unruly eyebrows. He'd known us and our family for years. He hadn't always been in holy orders. He'd been a teacher. Once, on the London train, I'd tried and failed to engage him in a discussion about a fine point of theology. I'd found him wanting in scholarship. At moments of great stress and urgency, it's astounding that such irrelevancies enter the mind. How, at a time like that, could I have let such an insufferable intellectual snobbery get in? *He'll have to do, he's all I've got*, was what I unworthily thought.

'Poor Lorna,' he said.

'That's not enough,' I said. 'Pray for her. Please, Doug.

I'm sorry about this.' I meant my weeping, my choked throat. I got back in the car to drive to the next church.

Ever afterwards, when I passed that spot, I was to think of him as he looked when I started the engine: holding his upright bicycle, standing in the gutter in his cycle clips, assembling a petition impromptu while ready-mix concrete lorries thundered past him, their drums churning round and round like monstrous prayer-wheels.

For several weeks, there was nothing for it but for her to have a thick white wadding square over the empty socket, held in place with sticking-plaster. In the M.F.U. surgery, after an initial squeamishness and repugnance, I learned how not to avert my gaze when the dressing was removed. Looking into that hollow was yet another loving intimacy I had of her. She lay on the tilt-back chair; the powerful lamps were adjusted, close up; I would hold her hand, sitting beside her or standing, while the nurse did her delicate work. If there is a very centre of someone's being, it is surely there, in the recess behind where an eye has been. I knew her now as well as a husband can ever know his wife. When the nurse hurt her – necessarily, as she teased aways shreds of dead tissue with the shining instruments – she would squeeze my hand, and I would try to earth her pain somewhere in myself. 'You don't have to look,' she would say, wanting to spare me. 'You can wait outside, if you like, until it's over.' She had said this before to me – many years before – when she had gone into labour and her waters had broken; and I had been quick to leave the room when the midwife came, and go to a part of the house beyond the carry of her wailing. Then, I had scarcely begun to know who and what she was; what happened to her body in illness or in childbirth was still not proper for me to witness: like seeing her on the loo or changing a sanitary towel; by the alchemy of illness, however close we were in health, we became other selves, out of reach. Now, although I guessed the nurse would have preferred to have me wait outside, she would have had to eject me. Sometimes we had to change positions. As I went round to the other side of the chair, I would see Lorna's belongings waiting

93

for her in a neat pile on the floor: her handbag, her book, the copy of *The Times* with her Biro clipped to it by the crossword puzzle, the Marks and Spencer raincoat (which I hated for its mournful khaki) rolled up like a palliasse. And I would catch the glance she gave me from her good eye, and I'd wink, and so would she, because she made this point of showing that she still had an eye with which to do so; and I'd think: anybody seeing this person in the street, in her plaid skirt and plain blouse and chunky sweater and flat shoes, would not take her for anyone remarkable. Then the probe and forceps would go to work again, stainless steel chopsticks inside the bowl of her head.

We went through this routine twice a week for several weeks, and seemed likely so to continue for ever. I came to feel as easy in the surgery as I might have done in the living-room of a growing acquaintance.

The question arose: should she have a false eye made? The prosthesis technicians invited me to have a mug of tea with them one day in their adjacent workshop, while Lorna was seeing the consultant. There was a long bench with stools, a Bunsen burner with a fish-tail flame, plaster casts of ever so many mouths, each inscribed, in uneven, black, felt-tip letters, with some stranger's name and initials. In this matter-of-fact laboratory they made ears and chins, pieces of forehead. An eye in a suitably encasing framework of false skin to match cheek, temple, brow and nose, would be no more than an ordinary challenge to these genial craftsmen.

At home, we talked about the question from both the pragmatic point of view and the aesthetic. The void had to be covered; the cover had to look acceptable. There were wigs you could buy (someone told us) with which you could make a waving cascade of hair fall interestingly over half the face, in the style of the '40's film star, Veronica Lake. We went to the wig department of a large store for her to try some on; each one made us laugh on account of its desperate artificiality. A wig simply was not 'her'. Well then, perhaps there were ways and means we could devise with, say, headscarves. We experimented, I holding a hand-mirror behind her while she sat trying several different combinations of knots and clasps and grips. It became unavoidably clear that there was nothing cosmetic we could do to disguise or conceal the fact of her missing eye.

'What do you think?'

I had dreaded this question, because I had known what I thought from the start, and was loth to tell her what she might find unbearable to hear. What I thought was that I had never once seen a false eye that had not made my stomach turn. I would have wanted her to have an old-fashioned, pirate's eye-patch: a plain black one, made of whatever would feel comfortable, with a simple elastic contrivance to hold it in place. Such a thing would be serviceable, quickly put on or taken off, easily replaceable and – making no bones about being what it was – less likely to draw attention than a false eye. Moreover, I thought, it would give her a jaunty, roguish air and quickly become a familiar part of her, a feature which might sit well with her new-found sharpness of wit. However clever the technicians were, however artful, however experienced in copying human tissue and flesh, making artificial eyes was not the same thing at all as making, say, artificial legs. Not only could an artificial leg be concealed from view inside its trouser leg; it also actually functioned as a leg – perhaps almost as well as the limb it replaced. A false eye would not see. Nor would it swivel, or focus, or dilate, or blink, or moisten, or cry, or transmit a feeling of love. Nor could the man-made materials and pigments that went into its making ever be convincing. The extent of human ingenuity, astounding as it may be, is finite. Tom Keating could fake a Samuel Palmer so well that experts in fine art were deceived. He could paint an eye pretty well exactly like one that stared out from a Rembrandt: but it was, for all that, only a painted eye.

'Tell me honestly.'

A technician in dissembling, I said: 'Maybe we ought to find out what they can do for you.'

'Apparently, they can fix the whole thing to the frames of your glasses. You need thickish frames and side-pieces, though.

A shame we've just spent out so much on these.'

She meant the expense of the new spectacles she'd recently acquired; the frames were delicate, feminine, fashionable. It was not like her to contemplate what she would have thought of as a waste of money; so, obviously, she had already made up her mind to have a false eye.

'They'll fix you up a treat,' I said.

Work began during our next visit to the M.F.U. The hospital photographer (I had no idea there was such a post) took a roll of colour film, shots from all angles. Measurements were taken. Then the senior technician, a gently-spoken, grey-haired man, brought in what looked like a tray of fishing lures. It was the range of available eyeball tints within the relevant bands of the spectrum, from dull grey to cerulean blue.

'Now, let's try to find the right match,' he said. And he began to select some to hold up, between tweezers, beside her good eye, to compare. The gradated hues were not named for the underwings of uncommon butterflies. They had simple catalogue numbers. One of these days, I thought, if I caught the man on his own again, I would say to him, not Chalk hill Blue but *Lysandra coridon*: more appropriate, when speaking to a man of science.

'By this time next week,' he said, 'we'll have made some sort of rough-and-ready mock-up. Don't expect too much, though – it'll only be a starting point for the real thing.'

'Quite,' I said.

'We won't be able to fix it to your specs, dear, I'm afraid.'

It was a question, week by week, of infinite small adjustments. I saw the object take gradual shape: a remarkable thing, like an exotic piece of taxidermy. The technician sometimes wore a green eye-shade like those one associates with editors in old American B-movies; he used powerful lenses, facing the natural light as he filed and sculpted, smoothed and modelled his creation. Before it was quite ready, with only her one good eye to see with, she had achieved the thousands of stitches needed to complete her needlework Prayer of St Richard. She signed it with her Christian name and the year, 1986, in red thread. I had it stretched and framed and glazed; and when I hung it in an alcove of the living-room, where it was to remain, she had a year and a few days left. The first time she wore her false eye in public was exactly a year and a day before she died. It was at a big gathering of the Walker family in a pub in Worthing. She had been in despair of ever getting the special adhesive to make the damned thing stay in place. 'I'm determined to show up,' she said, using all her fingertips to press the edges hard against her skin. 'All those people down from Worcestershire.' In a photograph of the event, she is smiling with all her face: her lop-sided cheek, her teeth which are no longer parallel with her lips, even with the wrinkles in her forehead and her chin; but you can't look at anything of her except that fake eye, with its steadfast, terrifying, penetrating gaze.

SIX

I HAD two pans on the go, with a couple of ounces of olive oil in each, just beginning to smoke. In one, I fried a kilo of seasoned potato rounds, and, in the other, two large, sliced onions. I beat half a dozen eggs in a bowl, added the onions and potatoes, poured the mixture into one of the pans, and turned the heat down low. In ten minutes, the *tortilla* would need to be turned over, to finish for a few minutes more. Then it could cool for half an hour and be ready to cut into cubes as *tapas* for my guests. I had already prepared a dish of kidneys in sherry and a platter of chicken breasts in orange and mint sauce, surrounded by miniature Martello Towers of short-grained rice tipped from a ramekin. And there was green salad and an avocado dip into which I had folded some prawns. No puddings: I understood that, these days, lovely women did not eat such things.

Four lovely women, in fact. They were renting the apartment above the Warboys for their holiday. Mischievously gratifying for me was the hooligan music they played late at night to enrage la Vicky, depriver of mail. Susan had spent some time with them during her stay. Three were about her age, mid- to late-twenties: Elaine and Samantha, executives of a record company; and Belinda, a television production secretary. The youngest, Kate, was a student from Australia.

I had discovered one, single, but not inconsiderable advantage of being a fat, middle-aged, recently-widowered man with a grown-up daughter in tow: being able to enjoy the company of a party of women, free from any strain of sexual tension. At the poolside, they had lain beside me on spotless towels, delectably uncovered as roast suckling piglets one might see brought to an adjacent restaurant table, filling the firm skin they'd grown into, newly-browned and moistly glistening. Many times in my life I had had to come to terms with situations encapsulated in the age-old stricture: *You may look, but you may not touch.* Within touching distance of this quartet, I had been enjoying a state of affairs in which I need not look – because there was quite obviously no question of *their* dreaming that *I* could dream of doing any damn thing else. To them, I guessed, I was a rather nice, harmless, funny, pot-bellied, oldish chap. I enjoyed this new status. For much of my life, where women were concerned, had I not sometimes tended to be a rather nasty, predatory, sinister, pot-bellied chap? Shamefully and shamingly I had often adventured, motivated by a vanity more swollen even than my paunch, a tomcat curiosity, and a rumbustious, buccaneering approach to every sensual opportunity life had to offer. I deplored this aspect of my voraciousness and what I did, or did not do, about it. I do not seek to justify it, excuse it or forgive it, beyond offering one piece of half-baked psychological theorising: maybe it was a predictable outcome of my having found my life partner, and sworn to be faithful to her, at the age of fourteen. Like many another wistful fool of the Sixties, I had been the culpable dupe of the new morality. Self-recrimination itself quickly turns into self-indulgence. Each of the four young beauties about to arrive on my doorstep had reminded me, perhaps by looks or gestures, perhaps by a detail as small as the curve of an eyebrow, of others much like them I had known. I surprised myself, rummaging for disremembered names, so as to compile a list to stand accused of – shoddy, enumerating Don Juan that I was. It was much too late anyway for such a document, too late for owning up, for understanding, for loving-kindness, for forgiveness; too late to beg for leniency, for clemency. What good would it do now, this new, ignoble, mental file? So I abandoned it, with only a grovelling plea to my bewigged conscience to take a number of similar cases into consideration, m'lud.

In mitigation (as I turned the *tortilla* and then poured myself a gin-and-tonic) I submitted that there had only been one instance of anything like a serious emotional entanglement. At the first premonition of the first hint of the first false dawning of the climacteric, my confidence temporarily shattered, my sense of failure huge as a hoarding, I had once been so besotted by a pre-Raphaelite-looking girl in a long white dress that I became convinced that my daft infatuation was love. It was the era of shoulder-length hair for men the age I was, and white suits and desperate shirts. I went off the rails, took alarming risks, courted daily disaster. I sailed her, like a brand-new yacht, into the fancied harbours of fashionable bars, eager for envious glances and blind to any disapproving eye informing me what kind of bloody fool I was making of myself. By the time I'd thankfully come to my senses, hurt, betrayed, ridiculous (and serve me right) I had even brought out a pamphlet of awful poems for her, of which I bought up every copy, immediately before publication, to destroy. (One of the most comical images I conserve of myself is of my ineptitude with the bonfire: the pamphlet was printed on high-quality paper whose ashes would not disintegrate; the burned print remained clearly legible; the wind lifted the pages one by one from the flames; I had to chase their flocks wildly round and round the garden, snatching them from the air, or cornering them in the flower borders like crippled ravens, so that I could despatch them with the flat of a spade and a gasp of *Nevermore*.)

'Afterwards,' said Elaine, 'we're taking you for a drink.' I liked Elaine. She was the freckly, auburn one who, having fair skin to protect from the sun, seemed demure compared with the others. She and Samantha worked for a multi-millionaire entrepreneur whose bristle chin, designer rags and actionable haircut had become well known following his undertaking to Mrs Thatcher to tidy up Britain. Samantha was more obviously sexy and outrageous; in the pool she had perfected the knack of floating, topless, while keeping a drink aloft in one hand and a lighted cigarette in the other. Belinda, who, on arriving at my door, had promptly fainted from the effect of too much sun followed much too soon by too much alcohol, was quiet, vulnerable, a dependable sort; not without Elaine and Samantha's powerful initiative, I guessed, but an organiser *for* rather than *of* others. Australian Kate, who was taking a year off from her medical studies, financed by daddy's credit card, I had seen move with the streamlined grace of a tunny-fish through the pool. She moved at times much like a tunny-fish on land, too, being gauche as the schoolgirl she had recently been. Though strikingly pretty, her face was not yet formed, still unwomanly.

'Yis,' she now said, 'you're coming out with us, right?'

'I've got plenty in to drink,' I said, 'and that's not counting all the stuff you brought.' They were flying back to London next day, and had bequeathed me a large carton full of their left-over bottles. A quick glance had revealed that the box contained nothing to drink: bilious colas, liqueurs named for Haiwaiian islands and Florida surfing resorts; bottles with pictures of bananas; one that was actually shaped like a banana; also something blue. All I had offered them with their meal was wine or water. 'Can I get you something from the box?' I said.

'You don't understand,' said Samantha, eating chicken with the same fingers as those that held her cigarette. 'We're going to take you for a *drink*. Explain, Belinda.'

'Down to Puerto Banús,' she said. 'It's just gone ten. Say we leave in half an hour, things'll be hotting up down there.'

I visualised Belinda with clipboard and stopwatch in studio or cutting-room; massager of egos of performer and producer, tactful booker of double rooms with double bed for solo married free-lances, repository of travel information, unsung but super-efficient maker of things to happen. I had worked most gratefully with her BBC sisters many times. Then I thought of the treacherously twisting mountain road down to the coast, followed by the murderous strip between Marbella and Puerto Banús. I knew, in that instant, for certain, that I was no longer suicidal.

'I'm sorry,' I said. 'I'm pie-eyed. I can't drive now.'

'Jeez,' said Kate.

'Elaine will drive,' said Belinda.

It had not occurred to me that, if driving were to be done, I should not necessarily have to do it; I had grown up in an era when it was assumed that it was men who did the driving. But I did know the girls had a hire car. The day before, they'd got me to change a wheel. It was still men who changed wheels.

'Maybe Elaine's pie-eyed, too,' I said.

'No,' said Belinda. 'Elaine's only been on Perrier.'

'You don't have to take me out for a drink. I've had a drink. I'm full up with gin and Rioja and I don't know what else. You don't need me. I'd be a right drag, your last night on holiday. Go and yak it up.'

'*Yak it up*,' said Kate. 'Jeez.'

'We want to say thank you,' said Belinda.

'For the yummy, scrummy meal,' said Samantha. 'I've not had a non-takeaway meal for yonks.'

Yummy scrummy, I thought. *Jeez*.

'And for changing the wheel,' said Belinda.

'Never mind all that,' said Elaine. 'It's just that we'd love to take you for a drink. No special reason. OK?'

I liked old Elaine more and more; it was true that I was tipsy, true that she was not, true that she yet might be before driving back from Puerto Banús. Like anything, I wanted to live.

'I've got nothing to wear,' I said. 'Just look at you lot.' Samantha, Belinda and Kate were in the casuals stylish that summer: the pink and pale apple-green T-shirts and pants that were the fashion cliché not only of the Costa del Sol but of every back garden from Surbiton to Giggleswick. Elaine, though, was in a starched white organdie dress, luscious. I'd bought nothing new for at least five years. Furthermore, until I lost two or three stones, I had no intention of spending money on clothes. From time to time I dieted, lost a few pounds; then lapsed, in a distress of compensatory eating and (more to the point) drinking. My wardrobe was comprised mainly of garments acquired at a small second-hand shop in Worthing that specialised in the jackets and trousers of the recently deceased. What I had on, now, was the kind of white shirt you'd wear with a business suit and a pair of Marks and Spencer lightweight slacks, *circa* ten years before.

'It really doesn't matter what you wear,' said Elaine.

'Matters to me.'

'Jeez.'

'Half a tick,' I said.

I went to the bedroom and took from its hanger the item I called my John Gielgud jacket: café-crème, of linen weightless enough to have to be anchored down with a stone if you were to take it off and lay it on the grass when a sea breeze rose. I put it on. Button and button-hole wonderfully met. It would do. I remembered how my mother used to say, when I was a self-conscious teenager afflicted with blackheads and embarrassing shoes: *Who do you think's going to be looking at you, anyway?*

I went back into the living-room.

'You can always pretend I'm not really with you,' I said. 'Or that I'm Kate's great-grandfather.'

Irony, in the ears of Australians (and Americans), can suffer the same fate as meringues in the paws of a baboon.

'I wouldn't say you even looked as old as my *grandfather*,' said Kate.

The horizontal string of lights of the fishing fleet became discernible from my balcony. It was what Eliot called the 'violet hour'. I could have done with being left alone with Count Basie tapes on the Walkman and my new bottle of Torres. However, there was nothing for it but to let myself be pleasurably grappled by eight nice arms.

And now, here I was, in a semi-stupor, in staggering dignity, in Puerto Banús. All of a sudden, I was transformed into a kind of threadbare playboy doing what Jimmy Finch had advised: *living it up.*

There can be few places in the world as comical as Puerto Banús. Its eponymous builder has created not so much a port as a gigantic carpark for the craft of the conspicuously affluent; a marina which might as well be a permanent dry dock: for the world's seriously new-monied classes seem to use it as a kind of rookery in which birds of their feather may live cheek-by-jowl, or rubbing-strake by rubbing-strake, in order to compare their several versions of vulgarity and show them off to a ceaselessly passing crowd of gawking hoi polloi. On the land-ward side of the promenade is an unbroken line of bars and restaurants; also shops of the garment-boutique persuasion selling, at prices zanily and cynically high, not togs so much as the postage-stamp size labels sewn to them in easily visible corners. The bigger boats seek each other out along the western jetty, too huge to rise or fall with the gentle roll the smaller vessels answer to; they are like bits of horizontal skyscraper somehow brought there and beached. Potted palms and heavyweight security men in parody maritime rig decorate their blazing decks after nightfall, while their masters and their masters' mistresses carouse ashore, at jam-packed terraces, often within ten metres of their own companion-ways. I saw a mushroom-coloured Rolls-Royce drive off the forward deck of one such ship and convey a freight of veiled, black-robed Arab ladies on a journey every bit as long as a cricket pitch. The car's headlamps were furnished with elegant little brushes which had been set in motion to wipe away any stray raindrops that might miraculously fall from the cloudless sky.

We had happily strolled along in the wake of this vehicle, looking at people who were looking at people who were looking at people, some of whom were looking at us. Now we ourselves were on a bar terrace: in an embowered, much-cushioned corner, under red plastic rattan. A waiter placed beer-mats in front of each of us. These were made as though from medicated lint, but scallop-edged and a good quarter of an inch thick.

'Quality,' said Samantha.

'What you like,' said the waiter, with an uninterrogative and challenging inflexion.

Elaine said Perrier. The others ordered rainbow-evoking

beverages incorporating salads of fruits not necessarily in season. I said scotch-and-water and emphatically no ice.

'No – have anything you want,' said Samantha. 'How about this place? We've come down here, most evenings. Glam – right?'

I tried to see it all through her big, contact-lensed eyes. Among the continuous procession, I noticed, were examples of what I supposed she might suppose were handsome young men. They were dressed in combinations of garments and embellishments which, had they been in vogue in my day, I would have thought the exclusive preserve either of young women, or the kind of ambiguous bloke you might encounter if you happened to enter a bar you hadn't meant to, perhaps in the vicinity of Old Compton Street: blousons and earrings, tinted blow-waves and elasticated pink head-bands, and such; their companions, if obviously female, generally had less allure – peahens to their peacocks. Uncomfortably they progressed in white high heels which met blue-jeans topped with, well, *tops*. Samantha was waiting for an answer to her question; and, for a few moments, no answer was forthcoming from me. *Glam*, I saw no reason to doubt, had a meaning for Samantha not unadjacent to the meaning I understood in *glamorous*. For me, glamour was a quality betokening a certain indefinable yet unignorable magic enchantment: perhaps delusive (as in the case of my pre-Raphaelite girl) but, in the instant, undeniable and utterly irrepressible. What I had seen, and what I now saw – and this through the muslin-effect of alcohol – was all too easily capable of repulsion. Oh dear. Youth surely ought to be, *ipso facto*, attractive. Was it my bereaved condition or my middle-agedness, my imminent arrival into old-fogeydom, that so alienated me? The drinks arrived; I winkled out the ice-cubes with my thumb.

'Terrific,' I said, secretly intending the original, literal meaning of the word.

Belinda had gone to buy an English newspaper. Now she returned; and while the four of them clamoured for information about pop music, I was able to warm my drink in cupped hands until it tasted of whisky. To adapt L. P. Hartley's dictum: youth had become a foreign country; they did things differently there. It was the people of my own age in Puerto Banús that I found more relevant to my immediate concerns: both those who were there to be looked at, and those who were there to do the looking. So many of the former wore the almost expressionless mask of jaded surfeit; so many of the latter seemed intent upon affecting that same mask, in envious or admiring emulation. Face after passing face I searched for outward and visible signals of forces that fired and motivated human life. What could one read in those eyes, and in the set of those mouths, of concupiscence or regret, wistfulness or deter-mination? Something about the immense, cosmetic artifact of Puerto Banús, its illuminated film-set imitation of an anyway mythical world, made those who visited the place put a clamp on their emotions; they gave away nothing of themselves: yet betrayed themselves by the very fact of wanting to be there.

'Not really your scene, is it?' said Elaine. The others were still engrossed in what they called the charts.

'It was a lovely gesture on your part to bring me here,' I said, 'and it wouldn't be very gracious of me to say I'd prefer to be somewhere else at the moment. I'm fascinated by all I see, I really am. I admit I'd not want to be part of it, but I wouldn't have wanted to miss seeing it. Got me at a bad time, that's all. For me, places tend to be an extension of the way I feel. And there doesn't seem to be much point to all this. But thanks for being nice to me.'

'We'll go when we've finished these drinks. I can guess how you're feeling. After all you've been through lately.'

'Forgive me. I'm not very good at dealing with people feeling sorry for me. I want them to, I admit. But then, when they do, I can't handle it.'

Samantha shrieked in excited disbelief at something she'd just read. 'Guess who's made it to number three?' she said to Elaine. 'Johnny Hates Jazz.'

'In that case, Johnny can go and fuck himself,' I muttered under my breath. Elaine was looking, apparently with genuine interest, at the tabloid page that had been suddenly thrust in front of her. Here was a sensitive, highly intelligent, well-educated and capable young woman having to take an interest in trash music records because they were her lucrative livelihood.

'Sorry,' she said to me, 'I didn't quite catch what you were saying.'

'I was just thinking what a shame it is that you're obliged to keep up with all that stuff.'

'A shame? Why?'

'Well — I imagine how you must hate it. It's all such worthless junk, isn't it?'

'No, I don't think it is worthless, actually. I love all of it. Well, nearly all. I believe in it.' She gave me a straight, but mercifully not too hard, stare. Then she looked towards the bill, upside down on its saucer.

'Won't you let me take care of that?' I said. I picked it up, and had time to see the amount before she took it from me, saying, curtly, 'Certainly not. You really mustn't mind a woman buying you a drink.' She replaced the bill on the saucer with getting on for ten 1,000 peseta notes. Forty quid for five drinks.

'Listen,' I said, 'why don't I get a taxi back, and you could all stay and enjoy yourselves.'

'No — honestly. We need to pack and clean up a bit. We've got an early start tomorrow.'

'Sorry to have been such a wet blanket.'

'You haven't been.'

'And I didn't mean to be insulting about the music.'

'You weren't,' she said, smiling broadly.

'Or the bill. Or whatever else.'

She drove us back up the mountain towards Cerros del Lago. I was sober enough by now to be able to enumerate my evening's tally of false assumptions, misconceptions and ill-advised judgments; not sober enough to feel as badly about them as I would in the morning. There was about a mile to go. I didn't intend to embarrass Elaine with any more apologies;

and in any case, the other three hadn't heard much of what had been said between us, so that apologies, now, would have to be tediously explained. Oh, I wished I could think of something positive to say about Puerto Banús: something I honestly believed, which could be said as a gratitude for having been taken there. In fact, there had been a wonderful, isolated object; one wholly admirable, unforgettable man-made thing. I made myself chuckle, imagining how ridiculous it would be if I were to expatiate upon it now. Suppose I said, 'Listen,' interrupting the chatter, 'listen – down there, I saw something bloody marvellous. Let me tell you about it. Right in the middle of that line of horrible great jelly-mould cruisers. Did you notice? A lovely old two-masted sailing ship – a ketch, I think it'd be called, but I'm no expert on such things. Whoever owns it has kept it in perfect nick – gorgeous, proper timber, none of your fibre-glass rubbish. I should think the rail was mahogany, some reddish wood, anyway, all polished up the way I remember old chaps' toe-caps used to be, ox-blood polish. And that royal blue paintwork on the hull! Twenty-two coats, I bet, and a shine deep as a mirror's. Not to mention all those handmade bits of brass brightwork. And do you remember that couple we saw taking a stroll at the end of the jetty? She had a face like a grater, but it was without any doubt her own face; and her chest had sagged level with her belly-button, but it had obviously done a good job of work in its day. And as for him: he'd had those cotton ducks for seventeen years, and they were innocent of designer labels, and long since ready for making rags for buffing brightwork; and his face looked as if it had been laughing and weeping all at once, and he might have been on the point of either pinching his missus' bum or pushing her into the hoggin. I reckon they were the owners of that ketch, and if they weren't then they should have been.' I would have got out of the car and made my way down my steps, but doubtless not before hearing Kate say, 'Jeez, what the hell was *that* all about?'

As it was, I got out, said thank you and goodnight and have a good trip home; and went inside, and poured a triple Torres, put a tape in the Walkman, sat on the balcony and stared towards Africa until I was beyond the capacity to cry.

★

Africa was where I went with Ed and Sheila shortly after they arrived; only for a day, only as far as Tetuan, only a few paltry miles across the Strait of Gibraltar: yet centuries away in a different world from the one which contained the obscene affluence of Puerto Banús. The Third World, in fact.

The ticket vendors for the ferry at Algeciras had been disinclined to offer information or advice about how to enter Moroccan territory from Ceuta. As soon as our taxi from the port dropped us at the frontier post, we understood why.

I am something of a connoisseur of controlled mayhem as an art form. There is a scene in one of the Marx Brothers' films, *A Night at the Opera*, in which perhaps a dozen people (though it seems like many more) crowd into a single, tiny stateroom on a transatlantic liner, all of them so intent – rapt, even – upon performing the several duties of their errands that they are oblivious of and impervious to their being involved in a zanily overcrammed situation. Such inspired lunacy had seemed pretty far-fetched until I found myself as an extra in a real-life (and totally uncontrolled) crowd scene as bizarre as anything that was ever dreamt up in Hollywood.

It began, as the best comedy should, fairly quietly, and with no more than the odd hint of the complications to come as soon as the Lord of Misrule has forged the first link of a long chain of hilarious logic. Truly as innocents abroad, we had left the orderly officialdom of the Spanish authorities' passport control behind us and walked the few yards of no-man's land, remarking upon the sudden squalor of litter and filth we saw and smelt at the roadside; and we had been surprised by the great numbers of vehicles waiting in several lines for entry: the Dormobiles and Volkswagen vans of returning *Gastarbeiter* mainly, their interiors and roofracks jam-packed with suitcases and shapeless, black-plastic bundles. Suddenly, now, we were entering an authentic Marx Brothers' scenario: *A Day at the Races* and *A Night in Casablanca* rolled into one, being confronted by an Arab with the build of Sidney Greenstreet, in stripey burnous and red tarboosh, playing Chico's hustler.

'I help you with passports. No trouble. No fuss.'

'We can manage, thank you very much,' I said.

'I help. You not have to wait.'

'It's very kind of you, but no thanks.'

We tried to ignore him, but he continued to walk beside us, not to be discouraged, every inch the thoroughly professional importuner. I muttered to Ed and Sheila, 'If we let old Abdul get his hands on our passports, we'd never see them again.'

His practised ear could have picked up a whisper from the far side of a football crowd. 'No no. I help. You need me.'

'Be a good chap and go away.'

'You English?'

'Yes.'

'No be trouble when I help you.'

'No.'

'You need me. Not many dirhams.'

'Watch my lips. No. No. NO!'

'You going see. Ha-ha!'

The passport control office was a long, low building with, as far as one could see, a single window embrasure about the size of a pub ashtray, calling to mind a wartime concrete pillbox; indeed (as Ed reminded me) Morocco was conducting a war in one of its thankfully more distant regions. Under and around the window, and clustered tightly to the wall in which it was set, was a gently heaving pack of about two hundred persons. The effect they made was that of bands of coral encrusting a reef, an image made all the more vividly accurate when one saw, from time to time, upwards of two hundred uplifted arms raised and waving in unison towards the window, like so many fronds of attaching seaweed being wafted by an invisible, underwater current. Drawing closer, we saw that this sporadic wafting was being occasioned by the appearance at the window of a hand. Closer still – now that we had, like fresh corals, joined the back of the reef of bodies – we could see that the hand was flicking out passports with the same action I used, when a small boy, to flick cigarette cards. Some of the hands belonging to the uplifted arms were trying to catch these passports: others were attempting to throw other passports *into* the embrasure over the heads of those in front; others still kept hold of theirs, preferring to wave or waggle them to attract attention, like MPs with order papers. Ed, Sheila and I opted for the latter method, though it was clearly the least effective; the khaki-shirted official within might pluck a proffered document or two, as a tiredly petulant fruit picker might snatch a couple of nearest apples: but for every one so garnered maybe a dozen fell like windfalls on to the sill. At first, the three of us tried to keep close together, binding like the front row of a set scrum at rugby. This had seemed a good ploy, our concerted forces perhaps able to insinuate us through gaps left by some fortunate and now withdrawing catcher. However, it proved not possible to bind tight with one arm raised; and in any case the set scrum quickly developed into a loose maul which flung us apart. We decided at once on a new campaign plan: whichever of us happened to be inexorably forced closest to the window would have the passports of the other two somehow delivered to him or her. For many minutes more, none of us made appreciable progress. We lost sight of each other now and again, drowners at a shipwreck. Ed's bemused face would surface here, Sheila's bob up there. We gasped encouragement to each other. Most of our fellow sufferers were Arab men, desperately but submissively obdurate, wearing the jackets of western suits over old-style, full-length, grocer's aprons. Others were young, and not so young, American women, ruthless, with honed noses and lethal, much-scaffolded backpacks. At the far side of the ruck, where the smallest and weakest were being ejected as by centrifugal force, a man had set a home-made ladder of rustic poles and rungs roughly lashed together with sisal. This he now ascended, carrying a bucket of whitewash and a paintbrush tied to the end of a long and evidently pliant bamboo cane. His job was going to be to paint the wall above the embrasure, reaching out with his bendy and dripping instrument above the heads of the wavers. Only minutes before I would have become a dappled thing, I managed to lob our three passports in, then catch them when (after an age) they were tossed out. And like a miner in a low shaft, I got my head down and stooped manfully through the dark to the periphery sunshine – where Abdul was handing a passport to the Frenchman it belonged to, possibly for not many dirhams.

For not a few dirhams, we negotiated a taxi ride to Tetuan. The interior of the car was not markedly dirtier than that of an English minicab and it was a Mercedes. From its window I saw men living with their assorted traps in the roadside ditch, or under bushes, much as I had seen men live in Lincoln's Inn Fields among the rhododendrons. Others seemed to be taking their belongings on indeterminate foraging journeys from nowhere to nowhere, like their itinerant London counterparts with their supermarket bagsful of possessions – except that many Moroccans had asses or camels to bear their burdens for them. I had read articles about the homeless and dispossessed I'd seen on the streets and under the bridges and in the shop doorways and parks and disused tunnels of England. The young among them had their reasons for being there: more often than not their inability to get on with their parents, their disaffection with the social structure. Men of my age, however, very often lived rough because three decades of stability in their way of life had abruptly finished with the loss of a wife through death or divorce, perhaps coinciding with the loss of a job through redundancy or closure; then depression, loss of confidence, drink, the slide into degradation by the attrition of hard luck's constant onslaught of demoralising shrapnel. Compared with them, I was blessedly fortunate, having a job and a house and a loving family; but during the instability of bereavement, I caught a candid glimpse of the kind of slot that my life, like anyone else's, might be forced to move along if another, and then another, and then another, bad thing should happen. When I had been a young man in my twenties, it had been unthinkable that a decent, reasonable fellow who had paid his taxes for thirty years should end up kipping in a cardboard box. Now it was becoming commonplace; Englishmen had lost what the Moroccans had never had: security, but with the acquisition of that security they had also lost the qualities of cunning, resourcefulness and dogged persistence without which few Moroccans could fuel their will to survive. In this sense, the fifty-year-old Yorkshireman dosser in Lincoln's Inn Fields had less going for him than the ragged Arab sitting with his legs in a ditch beside the P28 highway. Less, too, than the flocks of independent guides lying in wait for us when we reached the taxi terminus in the centre of Tetuan.

They fell upon us and attached themselves like kites to a carcass. You brushed them off, they resettled at once like horse-flies. At first, just one: some age between thirteen and thirty-three, impossible to be sure; wearing, of all unlikely garments on a hot afternoon in North Africa, a Crombie overcoat.

'English? I take you see castle.'

'No, thank you.'

'I take you see castle. Yes. Very nice.'

'No.'

By the time we'd gone fifty yards, three or four others had joined us. We sought refuge in a café. They waited outside. We drank our coffees and left. They tagged along. Others joined the procession. Some left it. We got mad. They laughed at us. We threatened them we'd complain. They laughed even more. We went into the tourist office. The assistant, however politely, laughed. 'They try to earn a few dirhams, that's all.' We went outside. They joined us again. I went and spoke, in French, to a policeman. They disappeared like flies in the winter-time. Aha!

Round the next corner, though, a new one.

'English? I take you see castle.'

'*Fous-moi le camp.*'

'You like to see *souk*?'

'*Váyate, por el amor de Dios!*'

'No – you English. I take you castle.'

'Nein.'

'You English. What you want? I get.'

Ed and I did a pantomine, pointing towards a policeman on the opposite pavement and nodding to each other. The man disappeared into a crack in the street, a genie sucked back into his lamp. 'With the next one,' I said, 'I suggest we look gormless and don't let him hear us say anything except "Eh?"' But it was no good. The fellow knew how to hustle in every Western European tongue, and was prepared to try every one of them. He had reached Danish before I pointed again and muttered the universally understood word, *police*.

We wanted to wander about in places where there might be no visible policemen. With the next one to accost us, I used some odds and ends of foreign words and phrases which, over the years, had been burrs hooked to the fleece of my memory. From my time in the Boy Scouts, I dredged up some Swahili: a tribal lyric I had once roared at camp fires. I would use it.

'I take you *souk*?'

'*Een gonyama, gonyama invooboo. Ya boo, ya boo, invooboo.*' What it meant was: He is a lion. No, he is greater than that. He is a hippopotamus.

'You English. You want see castle?'

'*Karushgaya mayashgaya.*' I'd got this from a Japanese film I'd seen at the Arts Cinema in Cambridge in the early Fifties: *Rashomon*, perhaps it was. The sub-title had read: Cut off my head, stamp on me.

'I take you where you want.'

After Cambridge, my friend Gordon Pugh had done his National Service in the Army, training to be an interpreter. He had taught me arcane and antediluvian Russian military vocabulary, the words for 'quilted grapeshot' and such; also, a complicated verb that meant, 'to cycle up a one-way street with the intention of walking back'. These now eluded me; but I could remember the chorus of a plaintive little Ukrainian love-song. I spoke it. No good.

'Come with me, plis?'

'No – you come with us to the *commissaire de police*.'

Now we cooked up yet another ruse: improvising a maca-ronic, comprised not of shreds of real languages but of some stateless gibberish outlandish enough to confound our next oppressor. But this, too, proved to be no defence against battle-scarred troops who had seen and heard it all before. We had a little success with simply shaking our heads sadly at everything they had to say to us, as if eagerly awaiting the first recognisable syllables of Tamil, say, or Twee. But by now we had somehow found our way unaided into the *souk*, where no policemen were but where, it seemed, all our tormentors of the previous hour had joined forces to taunt us. I felt threatened and vulnerable in that knot of narrow lanes, hemmed in by God knew what menace might be in the minds of our would-be but thwarted guides. It wasn't for me (I'd learned my lesson well and truly from Elaine in Puerto Banús) to affect to be protective towards the liberated Sheila, or my son.

'I'm scared as hell,' I said. 'Let's get back to Ceuta. Now.'

And we did that.

It had been a happy day, the more so because I had got on so well – and without trying – with my elder son. This brought me great joy. For years we had not always been quite at ease with each other: a constant sadness for which I had only myself to blame. Too often during his growing up I had been overbearing, too quick to crush his intelligence and personality with my own. It was futile for me to repine at this: the harm I had done had been assimilated deep into his forming bones. He had long since become his own man. All I could do now was respect his independence, and not swamp him with opinionated statements and embarrassing gestures of guilt-ridden retro-active love. But repine I did, despite my best intentions. Of course I was sure of his love; yet in my present state of obnoxious self-pity and self-centredness I found myself requir-ing from him that very warmth I had deprived him of – if only so that I would then have the occasion to demonstrate my affection and my need.

The three of us had a day in Ronda. During the hot drive

back, a terrible atmosphere gathered between us, the miasma of an unspoken rancour. I had no idea what was troubling Ed. I could easily have asked him, but chose not to. Instead, I withdrew into a sweaty carapace of general recrimination, luxuriating once more in the disgraceful and destructive game in which there can be no winner and only one player. That morning, when we arrived in the town centre, Ed had got out of the car and (as I thought) moodily stomped off on his own, leaving Sheila and me to trail along behind. I worked up some indignation at this, and made some pompous huffings and puffings about bad manners. Sheila was not in the slightest way fazed. 'Oh, sure you know how he is at times,' she said, 'he just needs to be on his own for a little while, he's OK.' It takes no more than a pinch of horse-sense to recognise, in those words, the authentic voice of devotion, understanding and patience; and, as one usually over-eager to claim knowledge of the workings of the human heart, I should have responded positively: besides – how very often I myself had gone stomping off in my time, needing space and solitude like breath itself. All day long I nursed my self-righteousness; and, as I took the wide curves of the mountainside road downwards towards the sea, the drive became a grim and unstoppable *dégringolade* of self-justification for my behaviour during a similar, and fairly recent, instance of coolness between Ed and myself. The brakes of my emotional control were failing again.

Not long after Lorna had acquired her horrid false eye and the confidence to affix it, we made a short visit to Holland in May, where Ed was working at that time. He went to a great deal of trouble on our account, arranging accommodation, driving us to see the sights of town and country, taking us out to meals and drinks and such. By the end of the week, Lorna had been able to feast her good eye on colourful images to remember for what was left of her life – less than a year by now – above all the Rembrandts and Van Goghs (she loved the *Irises* best) in Amsterdam.

As a special treat for our final day, we made a trip into Belgium to see the Ascension Day Procession in Bruges. Sheila had crossed the North Sea to join us for the weekend (Ed was living what I guessed must have been a lonely life in a Veldhoven flat, with a tomcat, Chas, for sole company). It should have been an entirely happy, memorable and culminating occasion: the spectacular, annual re-enactment of a ritual dating back to medieval times, on a brisk sunny day, against a backdrop of picturesque streets and buildings. Somehow, though, the atmosphere turned sour while we sat over lunch an hour or so before the action began. Once outside the restaurant, Ed detached himself from us in what I at once concluded was a petulant, unjustified and white-hot rage over God only knew what triviality. Now, just over a year since then, I was re-living my anger with him on that afternoon: how could he have behaved as he did? And when we arrived back at the apartment in Cerros del Lago, I absented myself, in a blind fury, in order to pay him out. How long I persisted in this folly of attempted emotional bludgeoning, I can no longer remember: one hour, two perhaps. I sat by the pool while I could be alone there; and when the evening bathers began to arrive, I drove up to Istán and sat in the carpark, shunning all company. It was a madness, in the sense that not a diatom of reason was informing my actions; the medium sustaining me was the purest essence of solipsism. Even when I had simmered down and returned to the apartment, I was still only dimly aware of the harm and mischief I was making. The sight of their packed bags brought me to my senses. I instigated a short, hot, fatuous row, found a way to apologise and be forgiven, asked them not to go; and, before very long, all was nearly as well between us as I could expect.

A little while later however (I was ironing clothes) I began thinking once again about that lunchtime in Bruges. The restaurant was packed, the waiters slow, and I fired off salvo after crass salvo of satirical comment about the length of time we were being kept waiting. It was an insensitive piece of misjudgment: for whereas all I sought to do was make us jolly (for in reality, I wasn't at all put out by the ineptitude of the service) the effect must have been to make my son think I was, by implication, criticising him for having taken us to that particular establishment: it was one he knew, having been to it before. I saw all now, literally, from his point of view, imagining myself sitting at that table opposite his mother, with me blethering my unfunny remarks. He only had a few more hours left of her company before she had to make for the ferry at Zeebrugge, to return to England and yet another operation before very long. We could much more profitably have remained where we were, the whole afternoon, even without as much as a glass of water to nurse between us. A son, when he is a little boy, is his father's rival for his mother's affections; when he is a man, and shortly to lose her, he needs to be more protective of her than ever. I couldn't have blamed him, now that neither of us had her, if he had given me up, after this day's performance, as a hopeless case. But as I was pressing the collar of my second best shirt and steam rose up from the iron, he touched my elbow gently and said, 'I miss her very much.' His face was etched with concern, as it had been before we trooped out to watch the Procession of the Holy Blood; but now it was a different concern, and it was going to be all right if I put down the iron and clasped him to me and said I loved him.

SEVEN

ONE MORE WEEK I would spend alone in Cerros del Lago; but I'd had enough of lotus-eating and was ready to get on with life again. I swam my lengths each day as usual, basked in the sun, read and wrote, cooked my dinners and ate them; then drank enough wine and brandy to enable me uninhibitedly to sing on the balcony past midnight. I chummed up with a neighbour my age called Lloyd, who had made a pile in the antiques business (only to have this pile toppled in the Stock Market crash) and who had the misfortune of being an ecstatic Hispanophile married to an Hispanophobe lady. I made the acquaintance, too, of a kind of latter-day (though landlubber) Ancient Mariner, whose ceaseless quest it was to buttonhole at least one in three of new visitors to the poolside with a blow-by-blow account of how and why he had retired from business, settled in Spain, and met and married his business-woman wife, a stately ship of Tarsus called Gerda. Gerda was a remarkably large (about one-and-a-third life size) but perfectly proportioned blonde; German, ursine, husky-breathed and ever redolent of mixed fragrances betokening sexual acts both recently, and about to be, enjoyed. Entirely to my surprise, I had a joyous, three-day romance with a young, available beauty who sold real estate and lived with her mother and her fatherless baby close enough to my balcony to be able to overhear my nocturnal serenading of myself: a liaison delicious but evanescent as meringue; easily digestible and frivolous, faintly absurd and with minimum aftertaste. Each of these encounters was a valuable experience in the course of my rehabilitation, for each one reminded me of the infinite variety of life's potential. Able to see clearly outside my sadness once more, I looked forward to going back to England and beginning again.

No investigation of the pathology of bereavement should leave out of account such glimmerings and false dawns of reinstatement into normalcy. For those of an inherently optimistic disposition, they can even be resplendent insights of hope; a final gleam of sunlight along wet sand at nightfall, to remain in the grateful memory during the wakeful hours. They can illuminate the abrupt glooms, too, many of which I plunged into on my return through Spain and France. The greater the grief, in my experience, the more likely it is to spawn baleful offspring in the form of major and minor disenchantments. One is transformed by bereavement; one is perceived as someone worryingly other than before, someone slightly freakish and difficult to get used to, like a new amputee. You sense this difference of perception very quickly, in the treatment you receive and in the way you yourself respond to it. For much longer than you expect, you remain a much-diminished person in heart and mind and bodily strength; and though you do not court sympathy – indeed it can be difficult to deal with – at the same time you find yourself nakedly vulnerable to the pain of its wilful denial. I was to be dismayed, during the prolonged interim following Lorna's death, by the insensitivity of more than one of those very close to me, whose companionship in letters or in person I yearned for and whose shared laughter and generously unstinted fellowship would have been welcome and supportive at a time when I myself had little left to offer in return. I was to be much changed, and permanently, by such instances; never again would I make the kind of demanding assumption I had done of certain loved ones, friends and confidants who, on the one and only occasion when it really mattered, I found wanting. I took my hammerings, bent to them; and though I emerged from the forge usefully harder and sharper, I much regret to have to say that I was thenceforth to glint horribly with a new cynicism: being leery, now, of giving myself up in unsparing friendship without keeping an eye open to the possible subsequent costs in terms of disillusionment. In middle age, you do well to hedge your emotional bets for the future.

Day after day I drove, falling more and more out of love with Spain: another, though small, disenchantment. I holed up in comfortless billets not of my usual choosing, in which I was, for all my fatigue, either not capable of falling asleep before dawn or, having dozed fitfully off, I was very soon disturbed again and again. By the time I crossed the Pyrenees, eager to complete another lap, I was exhausted to the point of hysteria.

I can't imagine how I allowed myself to take a route *via* Lourdes. I did so, however, and found myself creeping along in low gear past infinitely dispiriting lines of gimcrack shops that specialised in hocus-pocus totems exploiting any last-gasp hopes entertained by the terminally ill. Pilgrims were ubiquitous, in ragged, sad battalions: in wheelchairs, attended either by entirely calm priests or nuns or by moithered and frantic-smiling laity; else walking alone, or perhaps arm-in-arm with another of their kind. These latter were the ones who seized my attention. I recognised them by their unmistakable complexion; also, curiously, by their gait: for the sufferers from incurable cancers do seem to acquire a carriage and a demeanour which, for those close to them, becomes as instantly recognisable as those of, say, athletes or guardsmen or undertakers. They shuffled along: gamely, but betraying the defeat they surely acknowledged in their heart. Apparently, they were in search of something that might yet remain for them of earthly life; peering in windows, stopping along the pavement for breath or a wanly-cheerful snatch of conversation, just to make memorable something – whatever – of the actual moment.

So it had been for Lorna and me, during the brief recuperative spells following each of her three successive bouts of cryo-surgery, the summer and autumn after our trip to Holland. Usually of an afternoon, we would traipse the High

Streets, our unspoken convention being to accomplish an unvarying mini-odyssey of errands. This had the effect of creating the illusion of continuity, if not of permanence. It used to please her, in her phrase, to 'shuffle money' between one and another of our three building society accounts. None of these contained more than a couple of hundred pounds; each one represented some small stake in, or commitment to, the future: something to save for, whether a holiday or a new suite of furniture or – a humdrum but oddly reassuring token of days to come beyond the day after tomorrow – for the paying of rates, electricity and telephone bills. By this time I had guessed, but dared not think about it, that she had come to accept that her fight against the disease had turned from vigorous attack into an obdurate, hard-slugging rearguard action. The evidence was there in the unwonted vehemence of her planning ahead. We looked in the windows of travel agents to check the price of airline tickets to Australia. When she was quite better, she said, perhaps she would be able to visit her brother, whom she had not seen since the mid-Fifties. On another occasion, I stood beside her in the wool shop when she ordered I don't know how many skeins of a certain colour to be put aside for her in the special bin that bore her name. She intended to knit matching winter sweaters for all the family, she told the manageress; and, in that moment, I visualised myself one day going back to the shop, but alone, and having to cancel the order and say why I had to do so. Thus, the tenor of our frequent shopping expeditions was acutely heightened from the banal to the electrifying; what had once been mundane chores boring beyond belief – the purchase of pork chops, say, or settling up with the TV rental firm – became precious and curious activities, experiences laid mint and bare by subdued panic. For me they were attended by an extra distress, which Lorna knew nothing of until it finally became impossible to conceal. Cryo-surgery, the technique of 'burning' off tumours paradoxically by the use of ultra-cold, left in its wake a terrible stench of dead and corrupting tissue. Even outside in the open air, it was detectable from within two or three yards. Inside this invisible cocoon of foulness she lived night and day, unaware. At home, after she vacated one room for another, I would open furtive and tactful windows, provide sweet-scented flowers, employ aerosols and out-of-sight, stick-on fresheners; I was glad whenever there were powerful cooking odours emanating from the kitchen to overlay, however briefly, those hideously unpalatable ones that permeated every corner of the house. If, at home, I was ashamed of my nausea, outside I was disgusted by my embarrassment. What I constantly feared was that she should, on top of all her continuing trouble, be the victim of some stranger's unwittingly crass and cruel remark; how would I restrain myself from creating a violent scene if that should happen? An evening we spent in a crowded theatre was an agony. Then one afternoon, in the confined space of a supermarket lift, I saw that several of our fellow-passengers were exchanging glances, frowning, on the very point of comment just as the doors were opening. I could bear the tension no longer. In the street I babbled a string of wrong words in the wrong order. With much dignity, nobility even, she assimilated this piece of new knowledge about her condition. Then it was I who cried and who drove us home from Bognor Regis with the car windows open wide, as now they were as I accelerated up the valley side and away from Lourdes.

In the hospital there was a small chapel containing the odour not so much of sanctity as of reverential furniture polish. I never saw anybody there except ourselves; it was somewhere to go to be alone for a few minutes during the perambulating circuits I took her in a wheelchair of the various wings and floors and corridors, which helped to fill the visiting hours. The eves of operations, too, we went to sit there in companionable silence, hearing the trolleys clatter past, the floor polishers whirr and hum, and the bendy plastic doors smacking hard shut against each other, like someone petulantly slapping a side of bacon. So, by long custom, we went there the evening before her final ordeal of cryo-surgery. This time, however, I too was in night attire.

By one of those outrageous coincidences which no fiction

could sustain – but which occur quite frequently in real life – I was to have an operation early next morning, at the hands of the same surgeon, in the same theatre, on the same general area of the head, as Lorna. I had taken occupation of my bed in Men's Surgical, two floors below her ward; then I had been questioned about my medical history, asked to name my next-of-kin and told what to expect. It was a trivial matter: my dentist had discovered, from a routine X-ray, that I had an extraordinarily large cyst above my upper palate. There had been an exchange of correspondence between the dentist and the hospital M.F.U.; I had been able to sneak a look at my notes, and had been mildly disturbed to see that someone had suggested investigating a possible link between my disorder and Lorna's. There was none – unless it was psychosomatic: I could quite easily credit that, as a consequence of imagining Lorna's suffering over so long a period, I may have conceived and secreted a growth in my own head out of loving-sympathy.

We sat in the back row of the chapel, holding hands as we had used to do as teenagers in the Luxor cinema. She turned to face me, straightened the collar of my pyjama jacket.

'Who did you give as next-of-kin?' she asked.

'Well – you, of course. Who did you think?'

'We ought both to have put down Ed's name as well as each other's, shouldn't we?'

I remembered a time when we had sat side-by-side in a plane, taking off from Heathrow for New York. It was the first time she had flown. Our children, whom we had left in the care of my parents, were still quite young. She had said, as we taxied along the bumpy tarmac, 'We ought to have gone on separate flights.'

I had laughed then, and unwrapped a boiled sweet for her to suck; talked banteringly as the boosted engines roared and we surged ahead gathering speed and were suddenly airborne; and soon she was calm and appreciative of the cloudscape below our wings, its fluffed edges enchantingly touched with sunlight. All was unreal up there; no danger existed any more.

124

Now, though, there was nothing of comfort to say as she looked hard at me from her one eye.

'As a matter of fact,' I said, 'I put down Ed's name as well.'

'So did I.'

'That's all right, then.'

'How do you feel?'

'Not bad. A bit jumpy. Funny old business, this. I wonder which of us they'll do first?'

'We might see each other in the Recovery Room afterwards.'

'I'd love a whisky. Give us a hug.'

On the 707, when I kissed her for being brave, she had smelled deliciously of duty-free *Je reviens*.

'We ought to go back,' she said. 'They'll be wondering where we've got to.'

She was not in a wheelchair. If we came here again, she would be.

'I'll walk you back to the ward,' I said.

'No,' she said. 'For a change, I'll walk you back to yours.'

We mooched arm-in-arm along the route our trolleys would be taking us in the morning, attracting the quizzical glances of nurses going off duty, adjusting their cloaks.

'Guess who's in my ward?' I said. 'Old Johnnie Ball from the book shop. Used to sit with him at the jazz of a Sunday night. I wondered why I hadn't seen him lately.'

'What's the matter with him?'

'I didn't like to ask.'

'Oh.'

'See you when I see you. Love you very much. Off you go.'

Forty minutes after my pre-med injection, I was still feeling far from calm. I lay on my bed, plucking nervously at the strings of my gown, trying to will the euphoria to come that I had known several years before, just prior to my hernia operation. Then, as I had been lifted by porters on to the trolley and wheeled away, I had amused my ward-mates by spouting Shakespeare at the top of my voice: *Down, down I come; like glistering Phaeton/Wanting the manage of unruly jades.* I felt certain, now – having drawn some inferences from comments made by certain members of the consultant's 'firm' (though not by him) that, whether or not she survived this operation, it was likely to be her last: more telling than the delicate innuendo of their words had been the inflexion of a voice, the angle of a look, the betraying kindness of the offer of a cup of tea; small, well-intentioned tokens accruing to the formation of an answer to the question I perversely continued not to choose to ask. From a familiar, superstitious dread, while I waited for the steadying drug to take hold, I was sharply alarmed at the prospect of my being unconscious at a time when, as so often before, however uselessly, I should have been able to be with her in my wideawake thoughts, rooting for her survival. Our leave-taking the night before had been oddly perfunctory; she had entered the lift after our final embrace with the blasé assurance of the well-seasoned traveller passing through to the departure lounge a little while before take-off: with time enough to be on her own, to make a phone-call or two, to have a read and a snooze before yet another lifting away beyond the earth and, an ocean away, another ordinarily thankful return to it.

When the screen curtains were drawn aside, and two burly chaps slid what looked like punting poles through slings, making the litter on which to shift my bulk, still I was jittery; and they and the nurse who accompanied me of course misunderstood why. We trundled past Johnnie Ball's bed (I guessed he was a goner) and past the lift gates and the chapel door, the porters joshing and jocular and the nurse soothing but bossy ('Don't cross your feet, dear – very bad for you.') In the ante-room of the operating theatre, still much perturbed and agitated, I recognised – despite the masks and skull-caps and deep-green gowns – two pairs of reassuring eyes: those of Tom Hale, the senior theatre charge nurse, a quiet-mannered and thoroughly good man who had once been our next-door neighbour and was still our long and steadfast friend; and of the consultant, John Williams, the outstanding man in his field in all England. I was able to say, 'Take good care of her, won't you?' and to hear them say that of course they would, before someone out of sight took hold of my wrist, and did something to it, and I was abruptly transported to that black stratosphere where no more worry is.

★

Not until I attained Normandy, within reach next day of Dieppe, the ferry, and home, was I able to sleep round the clock. This occurred in a private, suburban hotel which, with its straggly garden, peeling stucco, blistered and immovable shutters, gothic mansard roof and dormer windows, might have been drawn by Charles Addams. At any other time, depending upon my mood and company, I would have found it hysterically funny, or genuinely terrifying, and driven on in search of somewhere less numinous. But the fatigue which swathed me like heavy subfusc stifled all emotion and desire save that of a yearning for oblivion. I entered a dark bower of laurels and euonymous, carried my bag up some steps to a door which, when it was opened, revealed an ageing lady made as though from papyrus. Once inside, I found gloomy, oversize halls and vestibules containing enormously cumbersome pieces of mahogany furniture, musty and faintly patinous with mildew. Perhaps nothing had been moved within the house for sixty years; its dust could have been the undisturbed flakings of occupants long since dead. I was conducted down some steps and along a corridor slightly below ground level to a beige room: and was abruptly and thankfully alone; wondering, but not very curiously, why the wardrobe door should yawn ponderously open the instant I looked at it. The bed-head was like the lids of two grand pianos, the linen was clean but damp to the touch. But, reckless of the threat of rheumatic fever or whoever might want to murder me, I burrowed into the bed's old minatory whiff of camphor, and passed out.

★

When I came to, I explored with the tip of my tongue the new hole in the roof of my mouth. It was unlikely, I'd been told,

127

ever to heal quite over; I should have to keep it clean, using a syringe tipped with a length of plastic quill. 'Like the little brother of Higg's apparatus,' I said to my ward sister, a petite Irish woman. 'And what might *you* be knowing about such things?' she said.

It was not long before I could get up, put on my dressing-gown and take the lift up to Women's Surgical. Lorna had survived, yet again; but now she was obviously drawing upon the ultimate iron rations of her stamina. Within a day, I was discharged and at once resumed my routine of travelling back and forth between hospital and home three or four times a day, bringing the nightgowns I'd laundered the evening before, and the savoury thick soups and soft puddings I'd concocted; and a desperate series of little gifts and bunches of flowers to create a cheerful novelty, a few seconds' interim of beguilement during the ceaseless pain she now increasingly, if mildly, complained of. Not long after Valentine's Day, the swelling promise of early daffodils appeared in the turf below the ward windows, though late flurries of snow lay between their spears, expunging the green of the grass. I took her on more wheelchair excursions, as well as to the M.F.U. clinic for her treatments; we looked out at the weather, and the people passing through it, much as we might have looked at a film made a long while before. One day, alone, on my way through the long, distraught corridors to the carpark, I turned a corner and bumped into the consultant. He was breezy and beaming as usual.

'So sorry, Mr Williams,' I said, 'I was miles away.'

'That's quite all right. How are things?'

'Well, frankly, they're not looking too good, are they?'

'Oh, you mustn't say that. I'll not have the Path. Lab. report until tomorrow, so there's no reason yet to suppose there's any malignancy.'

He strode off, and it took several seconds before I twigged that he'd thought I'd been asking about my own condition.

There were, as it turned out, six weeks of her life remaining. After one of these weeks had elapsed, the registrar asked to see me and my children in the ward office. He told us of several new deteriorations. The tumour had travelled to her lungs. When pressed, he gave his estimate of how long was left. As it was to prove, he was accurate to within one day. It would be a lie to say that I was stunned: all the same, no moment henceforth would be untinged by this new, hard, knowledge. There was nothing vague any more; nothing mistily imponderable about what was to happen.

I was at her bedside, every morning, soon after nine o'clock. If she was awake, we talked, went on short walks to the ward kitchen to make coffee or to the day-room, where we attempted the crossword puzzle. She could still do anagrams amazingly swiftly, even without seeing the clue on the page: 'Either *charlatan* or maybe *châtelaine*, if there's no "r" in it – how many letters, ten?' Soon tiring, she would apologise for wanting to get back to bed. Sometimes a kindly staff nurse would afford us a few minutes of privacy, leaving the screens closed around us so that we could, perhaps tearfully, embrace without the intrusion of the old ladies in neighbouring beds – one of them too prone to a sentimentally vicarious participation in our love, the other cruelly satirical of it. When the drugs overtook her, and she fell asleep, I would get on with correcting the proofs of my book or go into town to buy her whatever she might need: a size 2 ruled notebook from W. H. Smith's, a tin of talcum powder from Boots, a pretty new bed-jacket from the top floor of Marks and Spencer's; her shopping instructions were always thus precise.

The little notebook became a document, charged with pathos, of her final month. It was always readily at hand, either on the bedside cabinet or in her dressing-gown pocket. In it, she would record, with exact times, each passing event of the day: the drugs she took (she had her own abbreviations for tongue-twisters such as metronidazole and fluorcloxacillin); the visits of doctors, family and friends; meals and drinks; trips to the M.F.U.; the last few excursions in the car to go home or into town for an hour or two; concise reports on her state of being. Her handwriting, once so firm and neat, became increasingly wild and spidery; her spelling, once exemplary, became idiosyncratic. The ward sister gently suggested to me that, now the outcome was inevitable, she might be better off in the local hospice for the terminally ill: unless, she went on, I could look after her at home. This outraged me, but I suppressed any show of anger. The hospital *was* her home by now, to all intents and purposes; it was where she felt secure. She had still not admitted to me (or, I think, to herself) that she would not get better; being removed to the hospice would have caused her needless distress, and in the house I could not provide the skills necessary for her care. On two occasions when she spent a night at home, it had been beyond my power to summon up and exert the firmness required even to keep her from the possible harm of falling over. Potent cocktails of pain-killers, antibiotics and tranquillisers made her clumsy, oblivious and sometimes monstrously euphoric. She would insist on holding the cup herself, and so hurt herself by spilling hot tea. In the middle of the night she would lurch to the bathroom and, before I could force myself awake, would be on the point of tumbling downstairs and breaking her neck. I had no one, usually, to help me. My role, I maintained, was to be in attendance at the hospital every day, as often and for as long as possible, doing those things I best knew how to do.

'I suppose you need the bed,' I said to the ward sister. 'I can understand that. But so does she. It's only a little while longer. Please – can't you keep her?'

'Of course we can. We just need to tell you the possibilities. The choice is yours entirely.'

This interview put me into a new frenzy. I defended her right to stay where I knew she wanted to be, unashamedly currying favour with the medical and domestic staff. I helped when there was heavy furniture to be moved, was unobtrusive when treatment was to take place; I bought a box of dozens of pairs of tights for the nurses to help themselves from, and chocolates and biscuits; I washed up, provided items for the ward kitchen which, apparently, the NHS could not run to – a whisk, a milk saucepan to replace one that had worn out. In short, I bombarded them all with a last-ditch charm so that they would be incapable of turning us out.

She achieved one more outing. I wheeled her as far as the car, installed her, took the wheelchair back to Reception; drove us to a central carpark, helped her out. It was the first noticeably warm afternoon of early spring, with brass bands of daffodils, blossom in foam on the flowering trees, the urban chaffinches stridently pink-pinking – all the usual March-time indicators of optimism and hope, but this year with an irony and a poignancy I could scarcely bear. Infinitely slowly, we shuffled in step, arm-in-arm, through a narrow twitten to the pedestrian precinct.

'I think I'd like to buy a pair of pixie-boots,' she said. We looked at some in the window of a shoe-shop. 'Maybe not today, though.'

'How about a cup of coffee in Morelli's?'

'Lovely.'

She said she'd have a prawn sandwich, too, with mayonnaise and lettuce. While I queued for it, I thought of her entries in the notebook for the day before. I'd read it while she slept.

Tea	6.30
Metro 400 m.g.	6.45
Queazy	7.30
Breakfast, porridge tea	8.20
MST 30 m.g.	8.50
Pain	
More severe	9.15
Less severe	9.45
Dressing	12.00
Lunch Ted's savoury mince	
plums & custard	1.10
Elixir. Queasy	
B.P. Temp & pulse	1.20
Audrey	3.20
Tricia	3.30
Asp & Pap	4.20
Supper	6.00

Sick	6.15
Queasy	6.30
Sick injection	6.45
30 mils liq. paraffin	6.45
5 mils Asilone, Horlicks	7.45
Metro, elixir	9.45
MST	10.00

A constant sufferer now from indigestion, constipation and nausea, she smiled and nibbled at the sandwich not from an old pleasure but for my reassurance. She managed about a quarter of one half of it before giving up.

'It seems such a shame to waste it,' she said. 'Can you finish it up?'

We went back the way we had come not so many minutes before; and while she was put to bed, I returned the wheelchair. She was still asleep when I arrived for the evening visiting hour, and kept nodding off until it grew late. Well after the home-going bell had been rung, I was still at her side: by now I was allowed to come and go whenever I chose. The afternoon excursion had been too much for her. She was half sitting, half lying against her mound of pillows, as for receiving visitors, but her sleeping had deprived us of our usual chat. Finally, I put on my coat and kissed her goodnight.

'Do you know what I'd really like?' she said, her eyes still closed.

'No, love. What would you like?' I thought she meant those pixie-boots.

'Some chips.'

'Well, I must say – you're full of surprises! Salt and vinegar?'

'Please.'

The errand took a good half hour. The ward lights had been turned off. She was fast asleep as I sat down on the edge of the bed and unwrapped the packet of chips, releasing their sudden pungency. I gently roused her and asked, in a whisper, whether she still fancied eating them. She said she did, so I helped her to sit up straight. I picked a good plump chip and fed it to her.

132

'Eat up, now,' I said, 'you've always been able to put away some chips.'

Her eyes would not stay open. With an obvious effort, she managed to chew, then to swallow, the chip. I selected another, just as plump but much longer. She took it between her lips, without biting into it, her breathing both slow and shallow. I should have realised that she was trying to overcome nausea, but fatuously I persisted.

'Does me good to see you eat something you fancy.'

The chip dangled from the side of her mouth, bending with its weight. She looked like a fledgling too glutted to ingest the oversize lobworm the mother bird has brought for it.

'Just a little try,' I said.

She had said not a word; nor did she now. With a weary hand, she pushed the chip a little further into her mouth. Now it looked like a pale cheroot, its tip slightly darker than the rest. I waited, watching to see whether or not she would persevere. Only now did I understand what she had been up to.

The evening before he died in this same hospital, her father had sat up and eaten, with evident relish, the fully-ripe pear he had specially asked for. His chin had glistened with juice, and he had smiled expansively with the anticipated pleasure of each sliver of fruit that fell from the blade of his knife. Speaking his funeral eulogy, I had made much of this, emphasising that, right to the last, he had enjoyed whatever life had to offer him. He was a good sort. And now, ever her father's girl, Lorna was trying her damnedest to repeat his trick. I wanted, more than anything in that moment, for her to be able – for her own sake not mine – to open her eyes and eat one or two more of the chips and to smile with the old fellow's whole-hearted delight; but she was fast asleep now, with what looked even more like the butt-end of a stogie taking away all her dignity. I had long since learned how to steel myself against fleeing from signs of her suffering, to endure, to sit it out: but this latest version of what she had come to was insupportable. I was unable, from some new quality of fear, to bring myself to remove the chip from her mouth. I wrapped up the rest, called in briefly at the ward office to say she needed attending to, and then strode fast and cravenly away, deeply ashamed of myself.

Another day passed, and another. The little notebook journal recorded increasing pain and the doubling of her dosage of diamorphine; also, endearingly, the fact that Ed had made her a cup of coffee, and that she had, at 6.55, knocked over her glass of asp. and pap. and had had to 'start again'. I wrote some entries at her dictation, too. On my arrival one afternoon, before I had reached her bedside, the registrar told me that he would fix a diamorphine pump to her arm 'as soon as one becomes available'. This was the first I knew about such a thing: a kind of box which released diamorphine into the bloodstream at fixed, quite short intervals.

'How do you mean, available? If she needs one, surely — '

'Unfortunately, we only have a very few, and they're all in use. But I think there's bound to be one free before very long.'

What I understood from his expression was that some poor soul currently using one hadn't long to go before relinquishing it. I had no chance to press the matter: his pocket bleeper called him abruptly away before I was able to ask what the pumps cost. I thought wildly of how I would get in the car and go and buy one, the way I had bought a milk saucepan and a whisk. There had to be specialist shops where you could go in from the street and buy stethoscopes, sphygmomanometers and suchlike instruments over the counter. In London, certainly: just round the corner from Guy's Hospital, where the medical students bought their plastic skeletons and copies of *Gray's Anatomy*. Perhaps, if I found out the phone number of such an establishment, I could ring up, give my credit-card number and have a diamorphine pump sent down on the earliest train from Victoria. It was outrageous and sickening that the National Health Service, once the envy of the civilised world, should be so strapped for cash that my wife should have to wait for someone else to die before obtaining the easement of her pain. I had paid my taxes and dues. And, even if I had not, she was entitled. Anybody was.

I carried a plastic chair from the day-room and sat in it beside her, first waking her with a kiss on the forehead.

'How are you this afternoon, love?'

She looked at me, frowned, and took her time to answer.

'I'm in a lot of pain, and I think I'm going to die. What do you think?'

These proved to be the last words she ever spoke to me; and, as far as I know, I had just spoken the last words she heard me speak to her. I had nothing to say to help her; nothing that would not have been a soft, detectable lie: and I would not lie to her. So I must assume that she understood the truth from my silence, and she went back to sleep with me holding and stroking her hand.

When I went back in the evening, I found that a diamorphine pump had been attached to her forearm. The ward sister told me that she was unconscious, would not regain consciousness, and that she would very soon be moved into an individual ward off an adjacent corridor. I looked at the final entries in her journal. The handwriting was like barbed wire. *3.30 Box*, I read; *5.15 Still some pain*

There was no full point. Not quite, yet. Five days more, beginning with a weekend, she remained barely perceptibly alive in the side ward. If you watched very closely, strained hard to listen, you could detect that she still breathed. Our four children came with their partners; always, there were several of us present. 'Speak to her,' said a nurse, 'they can often hear what's being said, even if they can't answer back.' And so, one by one, we attempted impromptu, nostalgic, anecdotal monologues introduced by the formula, *Do you remember when …* But none of us, I think, found this an easy thing to do. Without a response of any kind, particularly when the sharp-edged flint of emotion forms in the throat and the eyes ache and throb, the words peter out; you look around despairingly for someone else to take over the baton; you curse yourself for falling down on the vital task. It was so little to ask: all that was needed was a familiar, much-loved voice to probe through the dark; the vocables perhaps broken up like those heard through a faulty telephone receiver. But the living and the dying cannot maintain a connection. Though 'they' perhaps can hear, we, ultimately, are left with nothing to say to them: but if 'they' could, indeed, hear us, and are offered nothing to hear, then that must be the most terrible and terrifying loneliness of all the kinds there are. I should have done better than I did, if only because I am a professional communicator. I have been able, very often, to talk into a microphone while I have been alone in a studio; and have had a sense of there being an invisible and never-to-be-seen listener somewhere receiving my message. I have broadcast on the World Service of the BBC, assured that 'they' can, and will, hear me in Brazil and Ethiopia; and, however unlikely this used to seem, as the engineers did their usual preliminary tests for sound level, I was able to summon up the conviction that the span of bridge I threw from Bush House was going to meet a similar span thrown to meet it from rain forest or desert. Wherever Lorna was, I simply could not believe my voice was reaching her. Just once, when I spoke low into her ear about the times when her dad and I used to go fishing together, and the hilarious incidents that occurred during our expeditions, she suddenly stirred and made a small, short moaning sound, and I almost persuaded myself that she had made an effort to respond. It was surely more likely, though, that I had interfered with her rest: for now she was the utterly spent lover no longer to be intruded on with whispers or inveigling fingers, no matter how softly caressing.

What happened – and at first this seemed bizarre, macabre, even – was that we turned our gloom into jollity. Now, if she could hear anything at all, what she heard was our laughing chatter. Our youngest, Bill, used his unselfconscious talent as an entertainer to make us, and to keep us, cheerful. He bore a poignant resemblance to his mother at the age: something about the brow and the hair-line, the way he held his head, his face when in repose. It struck me that I should always be able to see much of her in him and his siblings; and I experienced a ghastly perception of terror lest I should ever lose any of them. Billy, the baby of the family, had grown to be the heftiest of them all; he bear-hugged me nowadays whenever we met or parted and his deft, strong, mechanic's hand could impart a warmth and a reassurance into mine which I still felt in my grip for minutes after our handshake. I tried to arrange things so that he and the others could be sometimes on their own with their mother, in the hope that they might succeed in reaching her. Even if they did not, they would have their private words to say.

At night, I had a makeshift bed of armchairs in the ward. I lay in my clothes alongside her, listening to the intermittent click of the pump, stroking and squeezing her hand. Her pulse had always been difficult to locate, but I explored with my middle finger half the circlet of her wrist until I found it, feeble but continuing. There was an electric bell I could press to summon the nurse if I needed her, and I kept the cord of it close within reach. I sipped whisky and water. By the light from distant windows I looked at her gifts of fresh flowers and the little, ever-attendant clown, all of whose colours faded at nightfall.

I knew about the death-rattle: had heard tell of it, had read about it. In the darkness of the small hours it aroused me from sleep. I pressed the bell-push, switched on the lights, stood at the end of the bed. Like one who summons up a final milligram of energy to set foot at last upon a desired summit, she made a sudden convulsion, and the rattle ceased, and she was utterly still. I had never before seen somebody die: this was it, then, the greatest of all our mysteries. While I watched her stillness, two nurses came in and stood behind me, looking over my shoulders. One of them gripped my arm and whispered, 'She's going, she's going.' I was not deceived, though. She had already gone before the nurses arrived for what had been for them, I supposed, a commonplace event. 'You'll want a minute or two alone with her, to say goodbye,' said the second nurse. I turned to face them, wanting to say that no, as a matter of fact I felt weak and ill and wished nothing of the sort. The first nurse wore what looked like cake-frills on her head and at her cuffs; the second, an auxiliary in a drab dress like a shop-assistant's, had a kindly, peasant's face. I guessed I had to do what they expected of me, so I remained for five minutes after they closed the door on me. I was numb; and, at the edge of numbness, there was fright. Ever afterwards, I was to think it inconceivable that, in those minutes, I could not will myself to kiss Lorna's brow, or to say goodbye aloud or to cry: but that was the truth of it. When the five minutes were up, I telephoned Ed, told him the news and asked him to fetch me home. And, even back in the house, where others of my tearful family were ready to comfort me, still I could not cry.

★

Back in the house, after crossing the Channel and driving from Newhaven, I found airless rooms containing furniture and a smell of damp and decay. The house had become, so to speak, merely the place where I had used to live. It was a warm, August evening, still light, about an hour after sunset. I opened the downstairs windows, turned on the water and electricity and went out into the back garden. During my absence, an entire season had elapsed; a bed of summer flowers which old Jack Talbot had so generously planted were now fading, and the year had reached that mournful interim when there is no birdsong, and dust and disease have settled upon the rose leaves. On the way, I had called in at the village pub, banking on getting a snack. The place was 'Under New Management' and the landlord's wife told me brusquely that the kitchen had closed ten minutes before. No matter: I was not really hungry, and for all my loneliness, the last thing I wanted was company. I was not even going to phone anyone to say I was home.

I brought my luggage indoors and put away the car. I'd go to bed, I thought, and leave everything until the next morning. I had bought some whisky on the ferry, and there was nothing else I wanted.

In the bedroom I opened Lorna's wardrobe and stared at her clothes, and wept, and thought of how I should have to dispose of them. The wardrobe itself would have to go, too, as well as nearly everything else in the house: for I had no intention at all of staying on here – or in the village, or yet in Sussex, or indeed anywhere else in the country. Whatever the rest of my life contained, it would occur elsewhere. I would give in my notice at work and serve out my time; then sell up everything and, on the proceeds, go on my travels. So I had decided: it was the last of England for me. From time to time I would return to visit my family of course; but there was little else to retain me, and much to repulse.

The water was running luke-warm by now. I filled the wash-hand basin and had a shave, shuddering at the sight of flecks of blood on the wallpaper: sometimes, usually early in the morning, she would be just too late to staunch a sudden haemorrhage; she would spring out of bed to plug her nose over the basin, and I would see the droplets fly. They stained too deep to be erased with soap or detergent. Someone would have to paint or paper them over: not I.

I dried my face, standing at the north-facing window as I had always done since we moved in. The view was the same as ever, one I had once so loved to contemplate as I prepared for the new day. Beyond the lawn, the palm-tree and magnolia, the ten-foot, old brick wall, there's the corner of a wet field edged with hawthorn; then meadows, and arable acres, and in-determinate woods and the first slopes of the South Downs. On the skyline, claiming a hill-crest, is Halnaker Mill, the subject of one of my favourite poems in the language, by Hilaire Belloc. I called it to mind, staring at the mill in the last of the light.

> Sally is gone that was so kindly
> Sally is gone from Ha'nacker Hill.
> And the Briar grows ever since then so blindly
> And ever since then the clapper is still,
> And the sweeps have fallen from Ha'nacker Mill.
>
> Ha'nacker Hill is in Desolation:
> Ruin a-top and a field unploughed.
> And Spirits that call on a fallen nation

Spirits that loved her calling aloud:
Spirits abroad in a windy cloud.

Spirits that call and no one answers;
. Ha'nacker's down and England's done.
Wind and Thistle for pipe and dancers
And never a ploughman under the Sun.
Never a ploughman. Never a one.

EIGHT

WHAT POETS SEE around them at times of heightened emotion are the images of their inner landscape; all else gets screened out, as irrelevant. In the morning, wondering how to begin to construct a new life, I looked again from the bedroom window while I shaved. The sweeps that had fallen from Halnaker Mill in Belloc's day had been replaced, the primitive brick tower painstakingly restored; but, for all that, the building was still hollow: what it lacked was machinery essential for its functioning, for grinding real grain into real flour; sweeps the wind could set in actual motion, a fantail to face them into that wind, a post to engage a cog-wheel to turn a massive stone. It was a fitting metaphor both for a 'fallen nation' and for a widower. Even if I put the outer fabric of my being into good repair with assiduous attention to work, personal relationships and the day-to-day demands of domestic duties, what, if any, nourishing and satisfying staff of life would be produced by such cosmetic activities now that my Sally, so to speak, was gone?

I walked down Church Lane, wondering whether I might see old Jack Talbot at work on his allotment. He was not there; but Arch Simpson was, straightening out his potato patch after lifting his main crop, tossing the spent haulms on to his compost heap and forking the dry earth through as he went along. He must have been knocking on eighty, and had always been a fat man.

'Not letting the grass grow under your feet then, Arch?'

'Wrinkle I picked up from Jack. Get your ground ready soon as you can, look. Where you been lately?'

I gave him a summary of what had happened. He nodded, ill at ease. He plunged his fork in deep to use like a shooting-stick. A youth roared past on one of those moto-cross machines with mudguards two feet higher than the wheels.

'Sorry about your wife. Now I'll tell you something. What year was you born?'

'1934.'

'The year I got married. I was motor-bike mad, like young mooshtie there.'

'So was my Dad.'

'Engines, speed. All I ever thought about.'

'Before he married my Mum, my Dad went to the dirt-track races as a mechanic. Perry Barr.'

'Birmingham – knew it well. Liverpool kid myself.'

'But you sound pure Sussex – which is more than Sussex boys do nowadays. They all talk cockney.'

'Adapt – that's what you has to do. Came down, looking for a job. Found one, erecting greenhouses, met my first missus, got married, settled down. Took to the country, look. Used to have to drive a lorry up to Dudley to collect the hot-water pipes. Could never get loaded up straight-aways, though.'

'No?'

'Doooh. Saturdays, got there – see? Pipes stacked up like you might say terracing. All the blokes perched on 'em, shouting the odds, laying their bets. "Doh yo worrit," they said to me – that's the way they spoke – "we'm a-gooin' to stay and load yo up after, before we goos wum. Doh yo worrit none."'

'What was it – motor-bike scrambles?'

'Doooh! Cock-fighting. And all of 'em with their cocoa-tins.'

'For passing betting slips?'

'Doooh! what they brought their liquor in, look. One of 'em on watch, first sight of a policeman, they all drinks up and tosses the cocoa-tins behind the stack o' pipes. Bottles'd've been evidence, see? A cocoa-tin's only a cocoa-tin.'

He stared about him, squinting for something mislaid.

'Yes?' I said.

'Where was I? Keeps losing track, look.'

'Cock-fighting.'

'Not that. Ah – got it. Like I was saying, you has to adapt, as the saying goes. Now it ain't no business o'mine, and you can tell me not to prod my nose where it's not wanted, if you like. All I'm saying is, when my old Millie died, I set straight to and found another good woman, and never regretted it, and I'll do the same again if ever I has to, and take no mind o' what nobody else has to say about it. That's all. Said my piece.'

I watched him set straight to again on his plot, facing away from me. I'd have liked to know more about illicit blood-sports, liquor and gambling in the Black Country in the Thirties; but all that, Arch's back was telling me, was going to have to wait.

I continued along Church Lane; then, through the farmyard and under the lych-gate into the churchyard until I reached Lorna's grave. The mound I remembered of freshly-dug earth had settled. Old Jack had kept the grass around neatly clipped, and he had transplanted the rose-bush from the garden, as I had asked him to, as well as some pansies and forget-me-nots which he had thoughtfully and generously provided from his own garden. Somebody – one of my children, I guessed – had left some mixed cut flowers in a jam-jar; some time ago this must have been: the blooms rustled like tassels of paper, having shrivelled, colourless, on desiccated stalks. The jar was stone dry. I pulled up a few weeds. Now that I was back, I should take over the upkeep of the grave from Jack, of course, and see about getting a headstone cut. If I did leave England, who would attend to it then? I couldn't bear to think of it rank and neglected.

★

St George's had been packed. My children sat with me in the front pew. I had prepared the order of service, chosen the hymns and readings, written the eulogy for my brother to

143

speak; which he did very movingly: not dolefully, but in a conversational tone and with an occasional enlightening smile. I had had to be firm with the assistant priest. 'It's got to be Cranmer's Prayer Book, the King James Bible and Hymns Ancient and Modern,' I'd said. 'I'll not have my poor wife fobbed off with any of that gimcrack rubbish.' (A few days before, when he'd come to the house to talk about the funeral, he'd brought the so-called Alternative Service Book, the so-called New English Bible and a book of not hymns but so-called Songs. 'Ah, you are a traditionalist,' he'd said; and I had replied with some vehemence that there was nothing New and Alternative about death or the best language at our disposal to ceremonialise it. Too much of the power of the word and The Word had been fecklessly wasted by the reforming boobies. 'You mustn't distress yourself,' he had said, as though I was blubbing at the prospect of being denied something trivial, like a cup of tea.)

So it was that my best friend John Ormond spoke the unsurpassably beautiful first seven verses of the twelfth book of Ecclesiastes, and my best colleague Peter Martin read from the last chapter of Ephesians. They held the battered, leather-bound Bible which had belonged to my father and my grandfather before him. Both of them, like me, had been baptised Edward Joseph years before the ruination of the Church of England. John's Welsh poet's controlled orotundity exactly suited the rich Old Testament cadences; Peter's quiet, preppy, New England accent precisely caught the Puritan tone of St Paul's injunctions. We sang three of Lorna's favourite hymns, including one we had sung at our wedding, *Love divine, all loves excelling*. Throughout, the old words of scripture, liturgy and hymnal expressed what none of us present had better words for saying or thinking: words which, for the very reason that we could not readily understand all of them, embodied our awe and puzzlement in the face of mankind's timeless, inexpressible mystery; and which 'simpler' modern vocabulary and syntax would necessarily have distorted or crassly misrepresented with a presumption of lucidity.

144

We followed the coffin into the churchyard, past headstones of some of the Collinses and Bonifaces who had lived in our house in past centuries, bowing our heads as we passed under the lower branches of ancient trees, catching the acrid, ammoniac whiff of cowdung and piss from the adjacent farmyard, hearing the urgent lowings of Friesians wanting to be milked. We grouped ourselves round the terrible hole in the clay and saw how the wind caught the hem of the priest's surplice and fidgeted in last year's beech leaves, brown and stiff but still unyielding to the new season's buds. We saw the Shetland pony, Prince, put his head over the hedge out of curiosity at this sudden influx of people, and nod. We saw the impervious men from the funeral firm expertly slide the bands through their palms as the coffin was lowered. The ineffable deed was done as it had been done in the time of the great-grandfather I had never known because he had died too young. All that we did was right, and proper: the most, and the least, we could do. I picked up my handful of earth and crumbled it as best I could – though the wet clay wanted to stay bound within my fingers – on to the thud lid. The sky was huge and rinsed. A light aircraft passed not very high overhead and, half a mile away, a train sped along on the Portsmouth to Brighton line. Just beyond the boundaries of our gathering, there was an ordinary day in progress: the winter wheat growing, the cows entering the milking parlour, little children's voices carrying from the council estate, rooks not quite at rest at their perches in the high trees. Every sight and sound was super-real. You knew that this was one of those events every detail of which you would remember until your own dying day. I began to be aware of the stricken faces of my children, and of my mother and father; of relatives and friends, my neighbours, Lorna's nurses, my pupils, my colleagues, the President of my college, fond acquaintances, some villagers whose names I had, for that moment, disremembered; of some, even, who were strangers to me. I stood for them all to shake my muddied hand or hug me, and I tried to smile my thanks for their having attended, and wondered quite why it was that, though overcome not only by grief, and so much poetry, so many flowers, the insuperable beauty of the April day, the burden of so much received sympathy, the peril of my sons and daughters too young to be motherless, I was somehow still removed from the need of shedding tears that had yet to be shed. In a sense, I had done much of my mourning during the previous weeks and months, but there was considerably more to be done. 'Come to the house,' I said to everyone, 'I'd love to see you all in the house.' And for a little while the house was full while we ate our ham sandwiches and drank our Marsala and sherry. And then it became, bar me, empty.

★

In the empty house I packed a bag, then made a phone-call to Audrey in Yorkshire. She was still helping friends to run their bed-and-breakfast place; still occupying just one tiny room of their old farmhouse.

'They're very kind to me,' she said, 'and there's plenty to keep me occupied, what with preparing the guest rooms and the meals. There's the shopping. And feeding the goats. Running the dogs. Helping with the horses. But the weather's depressing most of the time and, well, I haven't got what you'd call a way of life. Not one I can call my own, anyway. How're you getting on, now you're back?'

'Awful. Got to get out of this place. Anywhere. Shall I come up and see you? Say no if you think it wouldn't do.'

'No – you come. Please do. It'll be lovely to see you. When?'

'Now?'

'Yes! I'll reserve a room.'

She gave me directions: straightforward, until leaving the motorway near Halifax, then complicated moves along by-ways and the edges of moors, through unremarkable stone-built hamlets whose whereabouts were known only to a few isolated fingerposts and shepherds; a far-off place away from home to be lost in, all but incommunicado, with just one person of my acquaintance whom I could bear to see. I contended with the aggressive and hostile drivers, slovenly and insolent service-station employees, awful snacks, unremitting danger, cacophony and ugliness of two hundred miles of the M1, thinking most of the time about Audrey's phrase, 'a way of life', and its implications. The way of one's life was directly determined by the purpose of it, its driving force; once this was gone, the former manner of living became an instant sham, an empty, cynical mockery, like that of a monk remaining in the monastery after definitively losing his faith. From the car window I saw spent coalfields, closed-down steelworks; and, not far to the west of them, I knew of the empty shells of textile mills: all former generators of prosperity when wealth accrued from actual stuff, and money was not produced mainly from fictions on paper. I passed, too, exits I knew led to theme parks and an entire anthology of the buildings, monuments and sites which, like John Wain's gorilla, bodies like the National Trust and English Heritage kept – with deadening hand, and mainly for the benefit of the middle class – not for doing anything but for being what they were. It was no longer merely a case of conserving castles and neolithic barrows and such; nowadays there were industrial and craft museums, tombstones for the industries and crafts fallen into the pathos and ignominy of desuetude. The last few miles of my journey, I crossed canals whose only traffic – between one immovable set of lock-gates and another – was a picturesque, horse-drawn barge giving pleasure rides; and passed countless little shop-fronts boarded up, whose proprietors had gone bust under the auspices of the present regime. Lovely England, once so vibrant, energetically productive, innovative, civilised and buoyant, had become an ugly, melancholy mixture of antiquarian peep-show and junk-yard; and very many of her people, with the stuffing (that came from making things) knocked out of them, were in the alarming process of exchanging civility for surliness and a new barbarity: characteristics now necessary, perhaps, for their survival.

I stopped at the last crossroads of narrow lanes before quite reaching my destination, and got out of the car. I could see the farmhouse, exactly as Audrey had described it, deep in the valley ahead, just above a small but heavy wood through whose trees the chimney-stack of a long defunct woollen mill protruded. After hours of traffic noise in my ears and the monotony of road-ribbon in my eyes, this halt was a balm. Yorkshire has a quality of deep greenness, in the low, acidic, registers, all but unknown in southern England; grass looks begrudged, the dry-stone walls accept lichens and moss and hart's-tongue ferns hostile to warmth; obdurate, betokening somehow a winning-back against the perpetual soddenness of their condition. A thin wind made an oriental music in barbed wire snagged with tufts of wool. This was all no more 'real' than Sussex; but the ruggedness, the asperity, the exposure, the very altitude, precluded all soft delusion. I breathed deep, relishing the cleansing air of an overcast early evening and, in a perverse manner, prolonging my solitude and the anticipation of ending it. I watched a tractor going home along a field-edge, trailing its cart. In the field behind the farmhouse below, I could see a black mare, her foal nuzzling her. I got back in the car, free-wheeled downhill close to honeysuckle and tall summer grasses, reached the ruined mill where the road still had its square and sturdy cobbles; and only then re-engaged the engine for the last few yards of twisting climb to the farmhouse driveway. Having entered this, I sounded the horn, got out, and waited a moment or two.

There was an exterior flight of stairs that led to a broad balcony and a door set into the floor above the basement stables. That door opened. And, as soon as Audrey came through it, I owned up to myself for the first time that – whether or not I had any business to yet – I already loved and needed her. What was more, I could tell from her demeanour that she was feeling much the same about me.

Only adolescent infatuation, perhaps, can appear as barmy and embarrassing in its description as the first manifestations of love among the middle-aged. Romance is the province of the mature young; and acceptable in the old because then it is endearing and thankfully free (from the onlooker's point of view) from the dangerous and discommoding connotations of sex. In persons of a certain age (even, or especially, *to* persons also of a certain age) it seems, more often than not, an anachronism at best faintly ridiculous and at worst comically undignified. Therefore, I shall spare the reader any further uneasiness on this topic except to say (maybe with a shared, indulgent grin) that Audrey, up on her staircase, and I, down on the lawn, were in future to think back on that moment (certainly with that shared, indulgent grin) as particularly special; no matter that – or perhaps even because – we enacted a kind of parody Heathcliff greeting Cathy scene: Haworth, after all, was nobbut a short gallop away over the moors.

In short order, we acknowledged what had happened to us. Also, that we were glad and grateful and deeply uneasy about it.

Wasn't it much too soon? John had been dead only nine months; Lorna, only five. What would they have thought of us? What would our children think of us? What would our parents and siblings say about us? What would 'people' say? Were we deceiving ourselves in our turbulent, volatile state, not unlike the way the newly divorced did, or hurt singles on the bounce? Was this seemly? Were we entitled yet even to think of the possibility of a new relationship? No, no, this was altogether ill-advised. It would be much more sensible to stay apart, keep out of touch, wait for a year or so to pass and then see how we felt.

But then: those who really cared for us would, could, only desire our happiness; would sympathise; would try to under- stand; and then – if this were the right word – condone; and then come to terms with the situation and give us their unqualified blessing. It didn't matter a tuppenny damn about what 'people' might say, of course: whatever we did was none of their business. And though – and fair enough – we still had plenty of grieving to do, probably for years to come, our turbulence was a state we had come to know the nature of, and time would irrespectively take care of it. We were sensible, level-headed and responsible people and we would discuss

149

every implication as often, and at whatever length, as necessary. Not without common sense, were we?

No, but – it stood to reason that ...

Yes, but – *Le coeur a ses raisons que la raison ne connaît pas.*

Thus we moithered, that evening at Farthing Hill, and thus we were to go on moithering for many months to come. I kept saying, 'It's all right. Everything will be all right, you'll see,' sure that this was so, but incapable – save by the strength of faith and conviction – of believing that it was. We sat on a small terrace overlooking a rose garden. Beyond it was a lawn bounded by a rather ramshackle fence; and, beyond this, woods in whose hollow ran the stream which had once powered the mill. I could see, above the crowns of the trees, a steep pasture in which a herd of shorthorn red cattle were grazing, continuously making a slow progress down towards the water.

'There's a broad pond about half a mile along the stream,' Audrey said. 'It's lovely there, completely wild, difficult walking. I sometimes go there. I must take you to see it.'

'Soon as you like.'

'It's a favourite place, And up there – ' she pointed in the opposite direction, over the lane and the field containing the mare and her foal – 'way out of sight, there's a ruined farmhouse. I take the dogs there. I want you to see that, too. You'll see why.'

Below us, but hidden now, the cows were audible. Occasionally one would low; but all the time they were making a restless movement, strangely disturbing, through the brakes and underbrush. The sun had not long set but; deep in that abrupt valley, darkness would never have felt far off, evening or morning, summer or winter. I had just returned from three months of almost ceaseless hot sunshine, an immaculate clarity of light; Audrey had spent those same three months beneath almost perpetually overcast and mizzling skies, nuances of grey. I had seen Lorna take eight years to die of her illness. Audrey had watched John take one and a half hours. Neither she nor I had felt able to remain in our houses, and we dreaded having to go back to them. By different routes we had reached the same destination. We fell silent, listening through the gathering twilight.

Then there was a sudden, repeated splintering sound, as of apple-box slats being smashed: a cow had leaped the fence and was lumbering in the rose-bed.

Audrey was transformed. A moment before, she had been quietly, languorously, meditatively sipping an after-dinner whisky, soignée and sophisticated in puff-sleeve blouse, slim skirt, heels, hair-do and earrings. Now she was the tough little farmer's daughter she had been long ago in a bleak corner of Lincolnshire. In short order, she had jumped to her feet, picked up a fair-size lump of gritstone, and, with a single, fluid, base-ball pitcher's action, sent it whizzing across twenty yards to the exact centre of the cow's flank. I had never before seen a dairy cow jump as this one did. It was up and over a yet unbroken bit of fence and invisible in the thicket, quick as a deer.

We sat down again.

'That was terrific!'

'Well – you can't mess about.'

Next morning, she took me to visit the goats in their parlour. They had been fed, and the nanny had been milked. As it was not raining, they could be put outside. Audrey led the nanny by her collar, and I chivvied her kid, Willy, up a stony path to a patch where the mother could be tethered. Willy had been castrated; he had a way of stopping and staring dreamily. Later that morning, I held grass on my palm over the hedge for the mare, Leila, who had bared her teeth at me for cluck-clucking to her foal. Then Audrey fetched the dogs to run. One of these was a big, inelegant young mongrel; the other, a subdued, spent, Labrador cross-bred bitch. We took them up the rugged way past the goats, along a splendid bank of hazels and alders where foxgloves grew in clumps as profuse as lupins in a herbaceous border; and then, past the last stile, we reached the upper, uncompromising moor of bad grass and bents and thin winds where stood the ruined farmhouse Audrey had mentioned.

It was a frightening place: a small, two-celled habitation, one of whose rooms a family would once have shared with their animals, and whose upper storey constituted not their sleeping quarters but an attic granary. All the windows were missing; one door was left, stifled by elderberry, on the sag of its single hinge. Outside, one glance at the hostile terrain was enough for one to know that there had never been a time when living here had not been utterly comfortless: small wonder that it was abandoned, left for ever to the weather. I watched the mongrel chasing a wasp, making a fool of itself, and was grateful for the small laughter generated by its lunacy.

'What I suppose round here they'd call wuthering,' I said. 'Bleak old spot and no mistake.'

'I often come up here. Suits me to be on my own – just me and the dogs. I've done my crying here, a lot of crying. You have to be out of the way of people to do that, don't you?'

'Yes, you do. You don't want anybody else round you. But it's different – you and me, I mean. We can help each other get it done, talk it out, cry if we want to. I think I would cry this minute, the least thing. You wouldn't have to mind if I did.'

'Of course I wouldn't mind.'

That proved to be indeed 'the least thing'. I went outside, swallowed hard, but it was no good. When I'd done, I said again, 'It'll be all right, you'll see. One way or another.' Audrey said yes, it would, and we started back.

We were awkward when we walked side by side. Audrey was shorter than Lorna; I was slightly taller than John. Not that we'd have been walking in step with our dead ones: but after thirty-eight years with someone, you have the ineradicable habit of their stride, the rhythm of their gait, the angle of their eye-line. I wondered, when we came to a stile, how John would have crossed it. Audrey asked me if Lorna had liked foxgloves. We talked about the two of them incessantly, and it was unbearably sad yet easeful to do so, using the preterite and imperfect tenses. Before we went back by the goats and the horses to Farthing Hill, we talked again and again across each other's tears, steadying each other, taking turns to listen. I loved my lost wife more intently then than ever; and also knew that which I would never have believed before: that a man can truly love two women at once; not in the same way, not for the same reasons, maybe, but quite validly for all that. It was going to be all right; and indeed it already was beginning to be.

'We'll go for a drive out tomorrow, if you can get away,' I said. 'We need a bit of time away from here. What you reckon?'

'Yes. I'll fix it up. You OK now?'

I was rubbing my eyes. 'Yeah. It's a bugger, isn't it?'

'Too true. A right bugger.'

'Tell you what, Baxter.' Baxter was her maiden-name.

'What?'

'You can't half throw. Not many women can throw. They put the wrong foot forward. Lorna knew how to throw.'

'I know she did, love.'

'Good-oh. Come on, then. We both need a whisky, right?'

'Right.'

We were both fond of our whisky. Next day, spent driving, we discovered the cascade of other shared tastes we hadn't entirely known about before, particularly in music: classic jazz, swing, orchestral works and grand opera. It was a balm for me to learn that she loathed modern jazz and pop with a venom matching mine. On the other hand, she was no more than coolly appreciative of the tape of Rocío Durcal's *boleros* which I'd brought back from Spain (and I must admit the sad, exotic love-songs transplanted uneasily to the West Riding); and I, in my turn, was disinclined to rave about brass bands: Audrey wasn't fanatical about the kind of music they made, but she had learned to play trombone with the City Band at home and was grateful to the form for having offered her, some years before, an *entrée* as an instrumentalist. I took us to Queensbury, not entirely as a leg-pull, so that she could contemplate that holy-of-holies of brass-banders, the Black Dyke Mills. Our arrival could not have been better timed. The instant we caught sight of the great, gaunt, blackened-stone factory, a violent thunderstorm was assembling. The sky had gone the colours of ripe and unripened damsons: purple, puce, ochre, livid-grey.

Closely adjacent to the mills there was a smaller building, whose ground floor housed a shop, closed at the time, retailing woollen products. We stopped in its carpark; and had barely sufficient time to ascertain that the band practice-room was above this shop, and to bow our heads in tickled reverence, before horribly close thunder-claps reverberated off the mill walls; and monstrous peltings of hail and film-set rain had us rushing back to the car. I put on a Placido Domingo cassette and turned it up to top belt to defy the thunder and terrifying, sky-rending lightnings. In that weather, and given our shared emotional climate, even the usually *pianissimo* passages of arias, heard *fortissimo*, were apt to our inner ears. We looked at each other's scared eyes with each operatic percussion of the thunder: sometimes laughing at the present circumstance and sometimes weeping at the past one, sometimes in synch with the other's feelings but sometimes not. When the storm edged away and the windscreen wipers could deal with the flung rice of the smaller hail and still spiteful rain, I drove to an exposed ridge high above where Manchester began; and there, in a lay-by, while we watched the sky become the gamboge and indigo of a black eye, and my little Fiat was rocked by mini-tempests of vast and close-rushing container lorries, we exchanged Donizetti for Tommy Dorsey's peerless singing trombone: calming, without a flaw, and evoking the years of the early 1940s before either of us was old enough to begin to know much about love or the ways in which it worked.

'It'll be all right,' I said: for the umpteenth time, admittedly; but the repetition was necessary, given that the words kept needing freshening, as cut flowers need their water changing, to keep them bold.

Next day, going back to Sussex, I was anxiously repeating them yet again. I had to attend at the hospital for my check-up, and though the hole in the roof of my mouth seemed to have healed satisfactorily, I couldn't help but remember the consultant saying, when we had talked at cross-purposes, that he hadn't been told yet by the Path. Lab. whether or not the biopsy on my removed tissues had revealed malignancy or not.

I went to X-ray, then carried my plates to the M.F.U. I handed them to the staff nurse, Liz, who greeted me for what I had become during the years of Lorna's illness: an old friend. She had been at the funeral, where I had not recognised her at first in her mufti.

She cast a cursory glance at the X-rays and said, 'Well now – have you been behaving yourself?'

I was much startled by this question, for it hit me like a reproach. Then I remembered that her words, couched as they were in the arch, euphemistical humour of her profession, only meant, 'Has there perhaps been any recent deterioration in your condition?'

I just smiled: rattled, and no mistake. Walking along the corridor, I had sneaked a look at the plates. The supernumary tooth in my upper jaw had shown up as an unmistakable, pure white shape about the size of a pine kernel. Elsewhere, though, there had been ambiguous mistinesses, somewhat troubling.

The consultant examined me and pronounced that all was well. I was too cowardly to ask about the biopsy. I told him I wanted to donate a certain sum of money to the hospital, month by month, to add to the contributions several people had sent to the house in lieu of flowers. He said that the pressing need was for a cryo unit, to obviate the need to borrow one from another hospital whenever it was needed. That sounded good to me; but I was keen, too, to obtain more diamorphine pumps. One of the wards, I had learned, had had to be closed through lack of funds. I hadn't much money to covenant, I said, but what I could spare would be made available in gratitude for all that had been done for my wife. I left it all in his hands. He said he would see me in six months' time. Another check-up, I thought, wondering why: but not caring, with so many other patients waiting outside, to ask.

Back in my unwelcoming house, I got a call from Audrey.
'Check-up OK?'

'All right, the man said. Leastways, for now. Wants another look at the hole in six months' time. I don't know what to make of that.'

'I'm sure you needn't worry.'

'Worry about every damn thing.'

'Maybe, if you made yourself busy – '

'Can't settle to anything. Million things need doing all at once. Too much to start on, so nothing gets done. Then I worry about that. Sort of paralysis. I ought to phone round the family, let them all know I'm home, but – '

'Why not start with Margaret?'

' – for some peculiar reason, I don't feel I want to see anybody at all. Just seal myself off for a bit. Margaret? Of course, you're quite right.'

Margaret, my younger daughter, like her siblings, was special and prized in her own way. As a little girl she had been (I had concluded, long ago, in a half-baked, child psychologist's manner) a classic sufferer from the 'third-child syndrome', battling to compete with her not much older brother and sister for attention and the recognition of her equal worth and attainment. After all manner of difficulties not her fault and not of her making, she had qualified as a State Registered Nurse; and, upon qualifying, had immediately published a long and scholarly article on blood pressure in *Nursing Times*. Then she had gone on to Sussex University to read for a degree in a modern discipline whose very title ('Cognitive' came into it) was baffling to one of my generation. When she knew her mother had probably no more than a year or so to live, she had taken time out from her studies in order to have a baby: in order, that is, for Lorna to see a grandchild before she died. Audrey had been wise and perceptive about phoning Margaret first. So should I have been; and realising this broke me up. I loaded the washing-machine, had a snack, a sit-down, and three fingers of strengthening whisky. Then I lifted the receiver.

★

It was a day of Lorna's last summer. Jonathan was a few weeks old. We spread a rug on the grass and made a picnic of simple things among the trees at Wisborough Green. While Margaret and her mother talked, I carried my grandson just beyond the reach of their hearing, and sang to him and spoke to him about the sunshine, and picked a leaf to stroke his cheek with. Then I carried him back and placed him in his grandmother's arms; and after a little while she placed him back in his mother's arms, and the two of us sat and watched him being fed.

She would not remember this for long, but would remember it for the rest of her life.

The baby was to gladden the ward more than flowers could. His father, Nigel, a patently good man to whom one could tell one's troubles, would rock him to sleep while his mother brought tea or quietly sat at the bedside, unable now, for all her expertise, to do anything more than the rest of us. Jonathan (but all of us left this unspoken) would not remember his grandmother; but he would learn about her one day: turning the pages of a photograph album, maybe, and asking who the lady was who looked at him hard and long from her good eye.

*

Obligingly he sat to have his photograph taken in the basket belonging to the inelegant young mongrel. Then we took him to see the other animals. Audrey showed him the goats; I lifted him on to my shoulders to inspect the horses over the wall. He had thick flaxen hair by now, and a robustly blooming complexion; he smiled whenever I asked him to. I picked flowers and grasses from the hedgerow for him to carry as he tottered along the steep lane. A cataract of love poured from me into him. Whenever he was in my presence I could not avert my eyes.

We went to Haworth and trundled him over the cobble-stones in his pushchair past shops full of souvenir gewgaws. While Margaret visited the Parsonage Museum, Audrey looked after him, sitting on the churchyard steps, until I returned from buying pies and beer for an *al fresco* lunch.

'She's a wonderful mother.'

'She's a wonderful daughter.'

She was wise beyond her years, I thought, as I drove us southwards home next day after Audrey waved us goodbye: a woman whose inherent goodness and humanity seeped into those around her as though by osmosis: without her trying, without her knowing. She was her mother's daughter, as her mother had been her father's daughter. When we stopped for her to change the lad's nappy and feed him, it occurred to me – without undue sentimentality or morbidity – that when my time came, there was nobody else that I would rather have among those at my bedside. She knew what to do and did it when it needed doing, with skill and caring and loving words. And she lived on fourpence a week, was 'non-judgmental' of her dad, had a son bonnier than a Glaxo Babe and dressed as though for a fashion plate, while she made do with kitting herself out from the Oxfam Shop. Soon she would take an outstanding degree into the bargain; and though she still ironically denigrated and under-estimated herself as she probably always would, she accomplished as much as the rest of us put together. No wonder our nickname for her was Grit.

There were a few days remaining before the new academic year began at my college. I took down the necessary texts from my shelves, blew the dust from them, *phuh*, and settled down to preparing notes. One of my courses was a seminar on the works of Philip Larkin. The message of his poems, 'Toads' and 'Toads Revisited', made a greater impact upon me than ever before: a job of work was what I needed now to help pass the time. I wrote down the final line of 'An Arundel Tomb' and took it with me to the monumental mason's in Worthing when I ordered Lorna's headstone. In a weird showroom like a set design for a dream-sequence, menacingly surrounded by urns and angels, samples of gaudy-coloured chippings, potted palms and pediments, crosses and kerbs, I watched the secretary copy out the line and then, at my dictation, the other details to be incised and set with lead: the name, the maiden-name, the dates. She wrote in blunt block capitals, counting the number of characters first from start to finish then from finish to start, like counter-clerks of old totting up the charge for a telegram. She handed the form to me to check. Pedantically, I inserted the acute accent in NÉE. It would have to be charged for as an extra letter, she said, OK? Next, I drove to the Imperial Cancer Research charity shop, parked outside on double yellow lines with my hazard lights flashing, opened the tail-gate and made several hurried journeys to and fro with plastic bin-liners full of Lorna's clothes. Of all the distressing things I had had to do, this was by far the worst: an ultimate act of disposal. Other possessions, such as rings, embroidered handkerchiefs and such, could be given to daughters or sons' partners; but garments, after a death, can seem like inauspicious totems. I had kept two or three of her prettier dresses, imprecisely visualising a time when the mysterious trunk in the spare-room cupboard might be investigated by a curious grandchild. When I set down the last crammed bin-liner in the shop, a supercilious helper asked me whether the clothes were clean. I could either have wept on her shoulder or thrown a punch at her. I fled.

Just before leaving Spain, I had sometimes been able to delude myself into believing that I had come through the blackest lap of my desolation. Back home, I was as if mocked and held in contempt by old routines, emphasising, as they did, the pointlessness, futility, fatuity, emptiness, of a life alone. Hypersensitive to every real or imagined hurt, absurd in the indignity of distress, I lost my self-esteem and then over-compensated for this with uncharacteristic belligerence and disdain. When I returned to work, my colleagues struck me as incompetent fools, my pupils as dolts: merely (I now believe) because they continued to perform their unremarkable functions as teachers, administrators and students as though nothing had happened to change the world for ever: how could they pursue such trivial occupations during an unlooked-for exist-ence on earth that Death laughed at, every second of every day, within touch of one's elbow? As it happened, some colleagues were indeed incompetent fools, and there are always a few dolts in the classroom: but I had temporarily lost my natural and professional qualities of cheerful tolerance and forbearance, and it was only when one of my pupils lost her father that my dormant qualities as a teacher briefly roused themselves. I listened to her and spoke such words of comfort (but not of consolation) as I could, without hypocrisy, muster; and perhaps they helped. On the other hand, from some deep well of bitterness and cynicism, I delighted in discomfiting my immediate superior, the Academic Dean, a youngish woman promoted from the faculty ranks. I have always been pre-disposed against figures of authority, admittedly: but instead of deflating her with gentle scorn and mildly waspish wit, I indulged in a campaign of flattening bombast and an overkill of venom. Also, I pilloried an inoffensive lecturer for his tunnel-visioned obsession with the land of his fathers. A deft and nifty bit of satirical sniping would have been in order: my persistent cruelty was unforgivable, as was my vindictiveness towards the Dean. I will not claim it as a general truth that an irruption of nastiness is a concomitant of bereavement; however, it is observable that dramatic, short-term personality changes often do occur, and can be as baffling and frightening for the sufferer as for the beholder. Before leaving the topic of behaviour and attitudes, it is worth recording that the newly widowed, like new prime ministers and presidents, are granted a grace period of a hundred days. Sympathy, or at any rate the avowal of it, is unstinted until three months or so expire; and then it is abruptly cut off. Or, if you claim that you are strong enough once more to face up to life again, people will be quick to take you at your word. The bereaved, like the disfigured, are embarrassing to deal with. They are unsettling, not normal. But I discovered that it goes beyond this, such is the perversity of human kind. If the widower should hint that there has come a new lady into his life, the sympathiser may well resent it: for sympathy is a power exerted over the mourner by persons who do not always understand how deeply they have been cor-rupted by it. They have, however unwittingly, an emotional stake in your continuing unhappiness, and it is disturbing to note that they may therefore go on being transformed by your grief long after you yourself have begun to recover from it.

NINE

I FETCHED Audrey home. It was towards the end of Septem-
ber; the woodland trees looked dustily tired, and the elegiac,
end-of-summer colours of dahlias filled the suburban flower
gardens. Her small house, about six miles from mine, had been
leased out to temporary tenants who had neglected to cut the
grass and trim the hedges. We carried her things in from the
car: her trombone, music-centre, suitcases, cardboard boxes full
of records and odds and ends. I sat at the table with a glass of
whisky while she went the rounds of turning on water, gas and
electricity, picking up the junk mail, grieving for her
unwatered indoor plants and noting instances of undue wear
and tear. The bath-tub had been damaged. It looked not too
bad, but was irreparable for all that.

'The place doesn't feel like mine any more,' she said. 'I'm like
a nomad.'

'I'll help you put away the clutter. You'll soon make it cosy
again. I'll go and get my motor-mower tomorrow and get
cracking. See to the privet, as well.'

'There's an electric hedge-cutter in John's shed.'

'Soon get it all back as it was. Sorry – that's a damn stupid
thing to say. Nothing will be as it was again.'

'I know what you meant. Don't fret.'

'I'll go and get us something to eat.'

The entirely round woman who kept the corner shop
opposite gave me a meaningful look which lasted from the
moment I entered until I left with a clutch of the kind of

dismally unsatisfactory groceries such shops specialise in.

'She's real nosy,' Audrey said. 'John couldn't stand her. But she was very kind when – '

'She reckons I'm after your money.'

'Why d'you say that?'

'I was seven pence short. Have to owe it her. I'm skint, till I go to the bank tomorrow.'

'Take a tenner from my purse. I meant to pay for the petrol.'

'Don't be daft. What does it matter?'

We ate the oldish eggs and thin-sliced white bread, and poured long-life milk into British Rail tea. Then we fixed up the music-centre and put on some pre-pretentious Duke Ellington.

'Make yourself comfortable while I phone Jenny and Debbie to let them know I'm home.'

Jenny and Debbie were her daughters, whom I didn't yet know very well.

I sat on the sofa where John had died. I would have liked to kick off my shoes and loosen my collar; but somehow it would have felt all wrong. John had always looked neat and dapper. This was still his house. In my house, Audrey would have felt the same: an interloper in Lorna's house. Worse for her, probably: men bought houses but women made homes. There was nowhere neutral for us, as there had been in Yorkshire. I stared at the furnishings until I heard Audrey hang up the second time.

'I think I'd better go home now,' I said. 'I'll phone to-morrow and we'll take it from there, OK?'

'Thanks for bringing me back, love. Not just the journey. I couldn't have faced coming in through that front door on my own.'

'Will you be all right now?'

'Yeah. Two or three whiskies, good night's sleep. Then see what's what, eh?'

I left her in the empty house and went back to mine.

She found a part-time job with a temping agency: part-time, because there was a limit upon how much she could earn without forfeiting her widow's pension. Sometimes, when she didn't know, I peeked at her through the louvred blinds of estate agents as she typed up lies about local properties. Early evenings, one of us would phone the other; I would cook dinner for us in my house, or she would cook dinner for us in hers. Whoever had to drive home afterwards couldn't have much to drink. We played Elgar and Bix Beiderbecke, Bruckner and Muggsy Spanier, Bach and Glenn Miller. Whatever it was, it could make us both cry – both the tipsy one and the sober one who had to go.

'It's a bugger,' I would say.

'It's a right bugger.'

And one night in my house – it was well into October now – I said, 'I can't stand being in this place on my own any longer. I'll get one of those sharks you work for to come and give me a valuation.'

'You'd do better to get more than one.'

'All right, then. Three. So – what do you think? Shall I come and live in Carlton Avenue? It's mad, us not being together all the time.'

'That's what I think. We haven't got a way of life like this. But are you sure? This lovely house. It has always meant so much to you.'

'It did. It does still. But it hurts me now, every minute I'm alone in it. Anyway, I need you more than I need it, and I can't expect you to come here. You know what I mean.'

'Would you really want to sacrifice all this? I'm not at all sure you ought to.'

'Ought to, be buggered. You and I have got to survive as best we can.'

'I know. But – '

'Will we hurt anybody? That's all that bothers me. I don't want anybody hurt, love. We've got to do everything right.'

The house in Carlton Avenue had been, originally, a bungalow. John had designed and built a staircase up to the attic, which he had boarded out and turned into a couple of rooms under the steep pitch of the roof. One of these had been his

163

draftsman's studio, with spotlights, a drawing-board with wires and pulleys and a cupboard full of plans and blue-prints and such. I installed my word-processor and the rest of my writer's paraphernalia, uneasy. I became obsessed with family photographs, Blu-Tacking them by the dozen to the walls and the low, sloping ceilings on which I kept bumping my head. I had long become used to having much more room to move about in; in Carlton Avenue I was a clumsy lumberer, a great dane in a terrier's kennel, often needing to go outside to stretch and shake myself. Gradually, with daily car-loads, I shifted more and more of my stuff from the one house to the other, where it looked strange and as though surprised. I gave some bits and pieces – Staffordshire figures, mainly – to my children, so that they could have mementos of the home where they had grown up. I sold some of my library at Sotheby's, including a 1785 *Complete Works of Voltaire* in thirty-five double volumes. The books had once belonged to the Sussex writer, Hugh de Sélincourt. I'd always had a sentimental attachment to them, having blued an entire week's wages when, as a schoolboy of sixteen, I had seen them in a Worthing bookshop on my way home after some heavy labouring during the summer holidays. I burned my bridges behind me every day that came: most of them were the simple, two-plank affairs of minor and easily reversible decisions, admittedly: but each of them a *ponte dei sospiri* for all that. One by one the valuers came to my house, made disparaging remarks about its several dilapidations, and gave estimates which differed by as much as forty thousand pounds. They would notice a rotten window-sill, the absence of central heating, some loose boards; I would see, in my mind's eye, the tumultuous images of twenty years of my life, both domestic and professional. But my mind was made up. I said I'd let them know, having already opted to place the sale in the hands of the purring Sloane Ranger who had suggested the highest figure.

I was deeply troubled. We both were. Being together was better by far than being apart and alone, but our grief still weighed horribly; and Audrey knew that, adjacent to my happiness with her was the lip of a chasm of gloom and something like madness. I was losing the sense of who I was. When Audrey was out (particularly when she went to band practice) I did little but study the albums of photographs which Lorna had compiled since our marriage. She figured in so few of the snapshots, having always been the one to wield the camera. I sought her from page to page. I wanted her back. I would close my eyes to summon an image of her, any image of her, in life; but at times, try as I might, I could remember nothing but the way she had looked in the undertaker's chapel-of-rest, as still as the lilies, in a dress not hers, and looking startlingly younger now that the lines of her pain had all been erased.

One night I emerged from a crunched-up, tormented sleep to the unearthly effects of what was to prove the worst storm in living memory: the Great Hurricane. The little house was being rocked by a ceaselessly high wind whose even more savage gustings slammed against the walls like sacks of cement hurled from a colossal ballista. We clung to each other, listening to the wrenched tiles sliding, expecting at every second that the entire roof would be lifted clean away. In the street, dustbins were being bowled clattering along, suddenly weightless as beer-cans. I threw on some clothes and foolishly went outside, thinking that I might attend to some battening-down, some damage limitation. The porch roof, of corrugated PVC, had been ripped away, leaving ugly snags of itself on the nails. An elm-tree with a bole as big as a man's waist – one of the very few to survive the Dutch disease – had been uprooted and chucked smack across the drive. Amazed, I saw it levitate, turn on its axis through 90 degrees and settle again like a fan folding – and then unfold once more, levitate, turn back through 90 degrees and settle again where the wind would have it be. I went across the street for a full view of the house roof. It was the ridge tiles and others round the chimney stack that had been taken. Overhead flew a continuous chunky blizzard of plastic bags, polystyrene, slats of fencing, underwear; also, more surreal yet, bladderwrack, miscellaneous jetsam, remnants of fishnet, oyster-shells and driftwood carried from the beach, a couple of miles off. The night was full of detonations, howlings, smackings and splinterings as masonry toppled over and trees were felled. I was hurled against a garden wall, like a wrestler caught by a sucker-throw. Grit and sand hit my face viciously as I staggered back towards the house, leaning into the blast at the kind of angle a circus auguste can in his long, weighted shoes. The last thing I saw before getting inside was an entire garage door floating and slowly spinning in a rising parabola, the way a frisbee does.

Audrey had been watching from an upper window. I must have looked like demented Lear on the heath. She grabbed tight hold of me.

'You might have been killed.'

'Something I'll never forget. I think we'll survive.' In fact, I was exhilarated beyond telling. 'Nothing to do but sit it out.'

By morning the storm, apart from the odd, petulant buffeting on the windows, was well past its worst. We inspected what it had done. As well as the elm, a good old apple tree was down; and so was much of the boundary fence. The ridge tiles were intact, having embedded themselves at an angle into soft turf, like a knife-thrower's knives into a target. There was a cache of spare tiles – luckily, because they were of an unusual, now obsolete, pattern – in the shed. I knocked up half a bucket of mortar, climbed John's ladder to his chimney-stack and made repairs there and then. And we were fortunate to get a man with a chain-saw to deal with the trees before lunchtime.

I was worried about my parents, twenty miles along the coast and within a hundred yards of high tide. The phone lines were down. We tried to drive over, but our usual roads were blocked with vast fallen trees. We found a different, circuitous route, passing bizarre, surreal sculptures: a set of traffic lights twisted like licorice, a fishing-boat on a bus-shelter pedestal. The old folks were safe, and miraculously little damage had occurred to their place.

We managed to get to my house. The day before, the agent

had wired his board to a brick pier beside the front gate. The wind had got hold of it full face, and the stout brickwork had snapped at a joint like a carrot. Several tiles and slates were missing, too many and in areas too tricky for me to deal with, requiring some scaffolding, maybe, and certainly a professional hand. In the back garden, the coping and top four or five courses had been knocked from several passages of the lovely, high, ancient, perimeter brick wall. One of the two Bramleys was riven down its trunk. The laburnum, which had always been leaning from the prevailing wind, was half uprooted, nearly parallel with the ground. The whole place looked forsaken: which indeed it had been only hours before, when it was put up for sale. It grieved me to see it so. Though I knew it to be sheer sentimentality to feel as I did about the property I had already relinquished in my heart, I wished these terrible things had not happened, let alone so soon. I was as though reproached by every spike of smashed tile strewing the paths.

In Bognor Regis there was shingle among the wreckage in the shopping centre; and in one of the parks, most of the great trees lay in criss-cross tangles, with dispossessed pigeons and squirrels cowed and grounded in the matchwood and frith. We drove to see the noble beeches of Slindon Woods prostrate, their massively wide-spreading root tangles absurdly exposed and clogged with clay and chalk and flints. Worst of all for a Sussex man was the tragic prospect of Chanctonbury Ring, whose eyebrow-shaped, hilltop landmark of trees I loved more than all others in the world, thinned to a smudge. My bit of England was destroyed.

A few days later I left for a week in the United States, teaching and conferring at the New Hampshire campus of my college. The break was useful, if only because it confirmed what I had sensed dimly though dumbly on previous visits to America: that I was a thorough-going European, more at home in La Mancha, say, than I could ever be in L.A. The languages I spoke – English English, French French and Spanish Spanish, rather than their New World progeny – were European; so were my cultural expectations and benchmarks. Deeply affectionate as I was of my American friends, I could never grow fond of the way they lived.

On the return flight, I wondered about where one could viably set up home now that England was done – owing, in no small part, to an irreversible trend of dire Americanisation. France, most probably: rural (if not urban) France might survive for a few decades yet the encroachments of a mentality and culture perniciously and inexorably suburbanising. Audrey and I might happily live out our days in a small house set in some unremarkable but unspoiled wine-country such as the Beaujolais, I thought: though, truth to tell, had I to see my time out alone, it would without doubt be in some unvisited *pueblo* in Castile.

Early in November, two of my books were published on the same day: *In Spain* and *Hands At A Live Fire: Selected Poems*. Of course it was the travel book which was most widely reviewed and about which I was more often interviewed on radio and television; it was short-listed for the Thomas Cook Award, though it stood little chance in a final clutch which included Colin Thubron's brilliant *Behind The Wall*. But it was the book of poems I cared much more about. Now that my spring of lyric poetry had dried up, I was glad to have the best of my work brought together and on the shelves again: most of my stuff had long since been out of print and, I guessed, largely forgotten. During Lorna's illness I had not written a line, and I had given fewer and fewer public readings. I would probably never have my name on a *Collected Poems*, like the Great Ones – or even many of the not-so-great ones; but my elegantly jacketed *Selected* would take its place in the British Library and be the titchy but traceable monument, if anyone ever cared to track it down, to something of which I was still proud, even though my petite Muse had deserted me, leaving me infinitely sad.

About this time, Audrey and I had occasion to pay a visit to the monumental mason's in Worthing where, not so long before, I had ordered Lorna's headstone. By an odd coincidence, John's brothers had chosen the same firm to fashion his.

Audrey had had no word from them, though work must have been started on John's memorial many months before. We parked, entered the yard. And there, facing us, leaning side by side against the wall, were the two completed headstones. It was one of those experiences straight from the pages of Thomas Hardy: one that you could never render plausible in fiction or, perhaps, even in verse. *Kind and gentle in all his ways* read the inscription on John's; and *What will survive of us is love* on Lorna's. We stood and looked at them for a long while. The stones were erected in St George's churchyard on the same day; only a few feet apart, just as they had been in the yard, but now facing the sunrise, as is the ancient custom.

Some people called Lawson came to view my house, and fell in love with it at once and forbore to haggle over the asking price. They were in their middling thirties, and pleasant enough. He was some kind of computer boffin, with an irritating habit of saying 'numbers' not 'figures' when referring to sums of money; she was plump and Earth-motherish, exclaiming in ecstasy when she saw the Aga and all the threadbare depredations she characterised as the old house's 'potential'. They had two children: a solemn little boy whose hobby it was to collect *tea-towels*, and his winsome sister. I showed them round the place, having first lit a log fire in the living-room, which I had also spruced up with some expensive, out-of-season flowers. I delivered them an impromptu spiel, mentioning for example the white-lady ghost the villagers had told me about when we moved in twenty years before, but leaving unsaid and unsayable what I felt. They moved from room to room in the house, then into the garden, then into the annexe, then back into the house. I'd had the roof repaired, but the garden wall was yet to be attended to. They visualised it all as already theirs, putting in a door here, knocking down a wall there, with me trailing behind saying that, if I'd decided to stay on, I might have done this, or had some other thing done, until I desisted, my musings cut short by the boffin's sardonic smile. 'I'll say this,' I continued, realising that he had me marked down as one who was all talk and no action, 'more than anything, this is a family house. It needs children it it, and a few pets.' What it would probably get, I was thinking, was Artex ceilings, Ercol furniture and double-glazing. But the conflagration was raging on the biggest of all my bridges by now, and I was positively eager to see its span collapse. The Tea-towel Kid was doing his best to douse the flames. 'There isn't a tree we could build a tree-house in,' he whinged. When his parents tried to stifle him, an action of which I approved and in which, whether or not invited, I would have gladly assisted, he whined, 'I thought this was going to be a family decision,' I found a thing to do. I would send the little bugger a sweetener, a tea-towel in mint condition. I had one such somewhere. It had OXO printed all over it; and, with a little ingenuity, might have made someone a makeshift garrotte.

Evidently the Lawson 'family decision' was taken in favour of purchase, for during the following weeks they made more visits, bringing tape measures, squared paper and sharpened pencils. They also sent in builders, plumbers, men from the Gas Board and the like, to work out estimates and provide 'numbers' for Mr Lawson's financial calculations. Mrs Lawson decided that they should establish their dining-room in the annexe. Since this would involve a traipse from the kitchen by way of the existing dining-room, a passage-way, the living-room, the entrance-hall and two steps down into and through a cubby-hole, I concluded that she had a notion of processional mealtime ceremonial not unlike a miniature version of what had once taken place at Versailles, complete with tureens, salvers and enormous, domed lids. It was – and it still is – unfair of me to characterise the Lawsons so satirically, for they were indeed pleasant enough people: but at the time of which I speak, a concentrated solution of bitterness and resentment was coursing through my veins; and though I had firmly made up my mind, I had clearly not so made up my heart, to up sticks. On the day that I had to attend at the house so that the Lawsons' surveyor and his men could prod, dig holes, scratch their heads, sneer and find fault, I stood with Audrey on the lawn and said to her, unpremeditatedly, and with a sharp sigh, 'I used to live here once.'

Christmas came, a festival impossible for us to deal with. Our status was ambiguous, neither of us yet subsumed into the other one's family, both of us burdened with memories of Christmasses past and their unrepeatable happiness. Together we visited, or were visited by, all our children and grandchildren: accepted as a couple by now, certainly, though not without an acute sense of awkwardness and strain on our part. In Margaret's flat, Jonathan was without a grandmother; in Jenny's house, Daniel, Mark and Lisa had no grandfather. We waited, ever on the *qui vive*, for the little children to approach us with affection when they were ready to. Early in the new year, my younger son Bill brought his fiancée, Jane, and his best friend, Dominic, to Carlton Avenue. I took Bill upstairs to see my room, my stuff, my photographs, all the evidence of my life as a displaced person, a *déraciné*. 'Have a natter with Dom,' he said. 'He needs you to talk to, now that Maureen's gone.' When his father had died, Dominic had been a boy, and I had kept an avuncular eye on him; and now that his mother was recently dead, even though he was a grown man, he was orphaned and virtually alone. It was touching, and a privilege, to be needed by him to talk about his circumstances and his future. But what I recall with more gratitude still is the way that Bill, in that desolate room of mine, made me realise not only that a man continues to need a dad, but a dad increasingly needs his sons to need him sometimes. My father had now attained the rank of patriarch. That was what I wanted to survive to be.

As January progressed, it became clear that all was not well between Audrey and me. The stress of dealing with our separate griefs while simultaneously trying to manage the reality of our present relationship and envisioning a shared future, was proving impossible to deal with. The oil of guilt and the water of joy would not be blended. Abrupt rows followed by prolonged silences became worryingly habitual. We grew increasingly tetchy. Audrey's once briskly decisive, pragmatic approach to life became more and more defeatist, off-hand, downright wishy-washy. I reacted by being more and more assertive, positive, downright bossy: to the point that one afternoon, in a street market, when I had been leading the way from stall to stall, she drew upon some ultimate reserve of her old drive, exclaiming, exasperated, 'I'm sick of trailing behind you all the time. You're too overwhelming.' Later in the day, I exacerbated the situation. We had bought a personal stereo with outlets for two sets of headphones. While Audrey was reading, I was listening, rapt, to some sublime music. Thinking that it would help to heal our rift, I asked her to listen in on the second headset; and when she declined to, I, like a fool, pesteringly tried to insist. 'It's so beautiful,' I said, while actually dangling the wires between her face and her book. 'Come on, you really ought to hear this.' 'Maybe what I really ought to do,' she said, 'is go up to Lincolnshire and be a dutiful daughter and see about looking after my mother.' So, while pretending to read, she had been imagining an alternative life in East Anglia much as, during my transatlantic flight, I had imagined one in Spain.

A few days later, I arrived back late at night from London (coincidentally having recorded a short, ecstatic talk on Spanish life for some radio language course) to have Audrey say, 'I've got some bad news for you, I'm afraid. The estate agent phoned this afternoon.'

Mr Lawson had had to withdraw his offer for my house, unable to raise the necessary 'numbers' to effect repairs and refurbishments demanded by his mortgager's surveyors. She embarked upon a depressing list of faults. I was not listening.

My relief, if not audible, must have been visible: for Audrey said, from concern for me rather than as one giving me my congé, 'Perhaps after all you'd be happier, back in your own home.'

I admitted this was so. Then, stickling for accuracy, I said, 'Not happier. But less unhappy, probably, yes.'

'We'll see how things go.'

'It'll all be all right in the end,' I said. But the familiar words lacked something of the glister of their old conviction.

We both of us wept. I could not be happy in her house; and neither could she, whether or not I was there. She could not be happy in mine; and nor could I be, alone. There was nowhere else to go. It seemed as though we had lost our chance, so that was an end of it.

I made several journeys to and fro, transporting all my belongings, including some shelving I'd bought for extra bookspace. I went through the small ignominy of phoning round, explaining where I was to be found henceforward, though not precisely why. I took the house off the market, defiantly standing up to the agent's languid persistence and pestering him to come at once and remove his board. At college, the new semester began. I taught my classes with panache, bombast, and shameless theatricality. I entertained my colleagues, filling them up with more than they wanted to eat and drink. I drank fearful quantities of whisky into the small hours, my silent toast being '*Contra mundum*.' In mid-February, I received an unexpected visit from the fragrant young woman with whom I had spent a dreamlike interim just before my return from Spain. She arrived on my doorstep, carrying an enormous bundle of daffodils in tight bud. I had never been given flowers before. She stayed for an hour or so. We chatted amiably about our previous summer's small adventure: but neither of us, we discovered, had travelled well. So we said goodbye like characters in a short story; and not until she had left, and I was looking for extra vases for all her daffodils, did I recall that this was Valentine's Day. I thought myself no end of a lad, but I was relieved she had gone.

Scarcely a day went by when I didn't see Audrey or phone her. She seemed so differently sad now, utterly a widow once more, fending on her own, temping by day and doggedly practising her trombone parts in the evenings. I went with her on a jolly coach outing to a band contest in Reading. I was happy to meet her old friends, including an agreeable retired couple – baritone-horn Wally and Mary, his wife – who had taken her into their home and looked after her with loving-kindness for a while soon after John died. I sat in the audience of the Hexagon Theatre to watch and listen to the band performing their test piece. Audrey looked tiny, vulnerable and most lovable in her band uniform amid a phalanx of large, whiskery, hearty, beery chaps manhandling euphoniums, E-flat basses and suchlike instruments unknown to the symphony orchestra and, to my ear, more in tune to the purposes of interior decoration – as occasional *jardinières*, perhaps – than for making music. The slide of her instrument looked much too long for her arm to cope with: but she managed it, as she was managing to construct, or rather to reconstruct, something of her former way of life. On the coach, coming home afterwards, during the inquest on yet another disappointing result, she said to me banteringly, 'A second-trombonist in a third-rate, fourth-section band – that's me.' One of her colleagues had just bought a brand new flugelhorn on a month's approval. I wondered whether, at my time of life, I could achieve an old ambition and learn to play jazz trumpet: but it was a forlorn hope. I was out of puff. I reminded her of the time when we sat outside the Black Dyke Mills in the storm. I wanted her like anything, for keeps, but it now seemed more and more likely that I had let another of life's chances slip me by, lost by default of perseverence.

Spain, once again, would provide me with a bolt-hole. Come mid-May, the academic year would be over. The very day after the college's Commencement ceremony, I would leave Plymouth on the ferry for Santander. During the long summer vacation, the worst pangs of bereavement past, I would be able to take stock once again and make decisions concerning what should be done about the future. As it happened, I had a sabbatical to follow: a year off on half pay. Maybe I could research and write another travel book to follow *In Spain*. I could explore the minor roads of Castile and Aragon at my leisure, tracking down the ideal *finca* I would recognise at once from my day-dreaming. If I chose to – lucky dog that I was – I could wander about Europe for all of fifteen months; it would mean sparse living, but I could subsidise my salary by leasing out the house which, despite Mr Lawson's surveyor's findings, was not likely actually to collapse. I booked myself and the car on to the boat, reserved a cabin. Then I phoned the Finches, on the off-chance that their apartment in Cerros del Lago still belonged to them and that it would be available to rent for a fortnight. And, hurrah, it was, Josie said. We settled terms, made arrangements about keys and such.

'Just one thing,' I said. 'Is there a washing-machine?'

There was a pause. Then she said, 'Oo noo. We thought it best.'

I phoned Audrey and told her what I'd done.

'Will you come with me? Some of the time, anyway?'

'I don't think I can, love. I'm committed to staying on through May and June with this firm I'm working for at the moment. Sorry. It would have been lovely.'

'Oh, all right. I understand.'

She thought it best, I supposed, the way Josie thought it best not to have a washing-machine. It was pointless to try to be overwhelming about it.

During the week's half-semester break, I had a commission to fulfil as writer-in-residence at a comprehensive school in Northamptonshire, a favourite county of mine. The week coincided with the visit to her mother which Audrey had long since planned. I guessed how her week would progress: the tentative proposal, tentatively accepted, that she should, in due course, become the live-in, 'dutiful daughter'. This, I began to feel certain, was the way of life she had firmly opted for.

'Fix it up for one of your brothers to meet us somewhere convenient on the A1,' I said. Her brothers, Derek and Graham, both lived not very far from her mother. 'On the Friday afternoon, I could be waiting at the same place to pick you up and bring you back. At any rate, the drive will give us a chance to natter a bit.' And for me to do some straight talking, I was thinking.

'Yes, thank you – that'd be very nice,' she said, and I could not relish her politeness.

Her younger brother, Graham, met us at a roadside café. During the journey, I had found no adequate words to entice

Audrey back. So, hoping for better luck on the return journey, I spent five mornings and afternoons talking and listening, in ugly, pre-fabricated huts, to tolerant children who had no urgent need of anything I had to say – and who were loth to say much about what they might have thought I wanted to hear from them. I was accommodated, in their lovely, remote house, by the lively and earnest Head of English and her dour husband, a groundsman who looked uncannily like Vernon Scannell and who, once I had shown that, despite being a poet, I was no piffling nancy-boy, accepted me as a proper bloke who knew one end of a cricket bat from the other. They fed me copiously; and, in my comfortable room, I nightly drank myself to sleep. During breaks between my duties, I sat in the car in unfrequented country lanes, staring through hedgerow gaps at the freshly-turned fields, where pheasants and rooks pecked among the furrows. I let the dwindling sights and sounds of immemorial, rural England come to me for the precious minutes left before I had to go back to another classroom full of youngsters for whom I was an antediluvian freak without 'street-cred'. On one such occasion, I listened to part of Nigel Lawson's Budget speech, and was all but definitively confirmed in my conviction that England was already a country hostile to the likes of me: a conviction further endorsed by yet another footling performance before yet another young audience I could not reach. Oh, well. I had, over the years, done several dozen similar assignments, when I had been able to drive away afterwards with a sense of a worthwhile job well done. All I had to do was accept that you necessarily reach a point in life when you must tell yourself how time, and time's changing attitudes, have passed you by. At any rate, the fee would take care of my ferry expenses: maybe even secure a few nights' lodgings and dinners on my way down to Andalusia.

On the Friday afternoon, Derek brought Audrey to the roadhouse, as arranged. I transferred her luggage into my car and our return journey began. We had been driving southward for a good hour, exchanging notes about the week gone by, before I said, 'Listen. About Spain.'

'Yes?'

I had prepared a well-reasoned speech, crammed with blandishments and irrefutable, if devious and specious, logic. It would have won over a Jesuit. However, it was unlikely to win over Audrey. And so, instead, what I said was, 'Bloody come.'

'All right then,' she said. 'I bloody will.'

We went back to our respective houses. On the anniversary of Lorna's death, early in the day I visited her grave. A dozen pale narcissi were in bloom, and a few pansies and forget-me-nots. I trimmed the grass surrounds and hard-pruned the rose-bush. The Shetland pony, Prince, nodded over the beech-hedge as he had done the year before; blackbirds and chaffinches were strident again and fierce in their mating-time. The new, viridian meadow grass was already lush. This was, perhaps, the spot I had come to love more than anywhere else on earth; this bit of earth (I would say so when I wrote my will) was where I would want to finish up. The church, farm buildings and farmhouse, grouped capriciously around a broad area of grass, were pure Sussex. They looked essentially the same as they had done for a hundred years, and they were hundreds of years older still. One of the church walls contained bits of Roman tile, fetched during medieval times from the ruins of a villa several fields off by a waste-not, want-not peasantry. In mid-summer, the doors of the ancient tithe barn, cocked up on its steddles, would be opened; inside, slightly snooty ladies would serve teas in aid of something worthy: and that was all right. It was all right, too, that the barn doors would be opened at mid-winter, disclosing, magically back-lit, a Christmas crib installed in a real manger, with real straw. Once a month from spring until the back end of autumn, the volunteers would come, bringing their own garden tools in their own barrows, to mow and rake among the graves of those whose line had petered out or whose surviving families neglected them. This was where you came when you needed to be quiet, to bring your unquiet; where, when your children and your grandchildren came to visit you of a Sunday, you went for your walk after a roast lunch and saw the cows

177

assembling to be milked; where you tiptoed with them through puddles and mud to peep into the half-light of fetid byres at the suckling calves, and the brooding, enormous, nose-ringed bull behind stout bars. This was the enduring core of the village: the true heart of where I belonged, whether or not I should some day desert it.

One step outside the farmyard gate, the perspective changed. From here, you could see the farm's further fields, which a proposed new major road would barge through; also, nearer, where the winter wheat was six inches high, you could see in your mind's eye the parcels of land where, if the farmer decided to sell them off, now that his wife had died, a thousand bungalows and terraced houses would rise beside banjo-ended cul-de-sacs. A few steps further on, and you reached the village pub, an eighteenth-century one named (surprisingly, in high-Tory Sussex) for a rabid Whig. This had been definitively ruined now, outside as well as within, by its landlord: he had grubbed up a pleasant little wilderness of hawthorn and field maple and torn up three-quarters of the garden grass where once you enjoyed your pint of a summer's evening, watching the bats and the stag-beetles fly; it had become all asphalt, a carpark fenced and gated outside licensing hours and patrolled by alsatians. To the pub came not 'regulars' so much as mobile drinkers promiscuous with their patronage, the majority of whom were as unprepossessing as their host. Close by, there was the Rectory, converted into flatlets now and all but unrecognisable since its lofty trees, interlaced with rookeries, got brought down. All along the village's footpaths and twittens, you could glimpse acres of abandoned orchard, ramshackle glasshouses collapsed into their rot, modest small-holdings gone ruinous now and for which planning permission was being sought and granted week by week. Skips got filled to the brim with the last vestiges of nice flint walls, thatch and lath-and-plaster, to be borne away to the dump; while millions of bricks and tiles not the colours of our local clay were brought in to infill those few remaining tangled places where little boys once made their camps and where, when little girls

178

joined in, they conducted their first, curious, magical, necessary explorations.

I came within sight of my house: black and white, plain, its sashes, window-bars and centrally-placed porch, front door and line of narcissi along the low garden wall making it the pattern for a child's drawing. I remembered a photograph of it I'd seen, taken from the same vantage in mid-Victorian days, about the time of Kilvert. There had been a mounting-post by the front gate; and the then occupant, one of the Collinses, had been snapped standing beside it, wearing a black frock coat and one of those broad-brimmed hats much favoured by curates. He was holding the bridle of his mare. The villagers had dubbed him 'Fancy' Collins, I'd learned, maybe on account of what the obituary writers to this day would euphemistically express as his 'not having married'. Fancy was responsible for the aged of the parish. When they became too old and infirm to labour in the village workhouse (which still stands: a doctor lives there now) they were removed to the almshouse of a small town twelve miles away across the Downs, the wives forcibly separated from their husbands. When they died, they had to be brought back for burial in St George's churchyard. It was Fancy's task to fetch the corpses in their coffins with a horse and trap, for a pauper's burial. It had been known for him (he liked his drink) to arrive at his – at my – house only to discover, to his sober mortification, that the load had slid off the back of the trap during his pixilated ascent of Bury Hill.

The house was called Myrtle Cottage in Fancy's day. The village 'square' it faced then had been a simple, long, treeless and grassless triangle which separated three divagating lanes. Looking to his right, past his thatched stable (the house, too, was thatched then) he could see the smithy; opposite him was the shop, the bakery, the granary, the malting-house; to his left, little but agricultural buildings, orchard country and arable land worked by teams of horses. In all, there were no more than about three dozen houses and cottages in the somnolent village, and scarcely any wheeled traffic apart from farm carts and the squire's carriage. There was no need for signposts. Not long

179

after Fancy died – which is to say, twenty years before I was born – the Great War occurred. Soon afterwards, the bareness of the square was relieved by our hefty War Memorial, surmounted with a curly-tailed lion and inscribed with the names of the twenty-six men who had fallen. Also, a commemorative elm tree was planted: one of three such, in widespread villages exactly sixty miles from London. The shop, which became known as the Elm Tree Stores, still bears the name.

Since I came to the house, the great hallowed elm, in which children liked to perch, has gone. So has its successor, the plane tree which was broken by the hurricane. In their place, the Highways Department have planted not an English tree but some copper-leafed exotic which would look nice in a stockbroker's garden in Purley. It is surrounded in the Square by fifty-six items of street furniture: lampposts, bus stops, telegraph poles, traffic information, direction indicators, warning signs, bollards, hydrant markers and the like; not to mention the white-painted, sometimes continuous and sometimes broken-line lane dividers and arrows on the tarmac surface. Traffic ceaselessly passes all day and most of the night: container trucks longer than a terrace of farmworkers' cottages; ready-mix concrete lorries; car transporters; trade vans; banshee-wailing fire engines, ambulances and police vehicles; over-revving, needlessly gear-changing Japanese two-stroke machines piloted by spotty learners; male reps in white fleet Fords with red writing on them, all coat hangers and portable phones; pop-blaring, clapped-out camper-vans toting sailboards; even, and frequently, a hooting hearse late for the crematorium. It's a far cry from the occasional whinny of Fancy's pony and the gritty sound of his iron-bound wheels in the lane. But it's a far cry, too, from a quarter of a century ago, when this was still recognisable as a place with its own – still rural, just – identity and integrity; peaceable, peaceful. Once a year, on Armistice Sunday, the traffic stops, held up by reluctant policemen while a short service is held around the curly-tailed lion. Stops: but engines are kept running for the quick getaway. There is no two minutes' silence. There is never quietness, let alone silence. And the sodium streetlamps burn all night long and allow no darkness. In perpetual light, flowers have only a short season to bloom.

In another five years, the village would be a thoroughly hellish place, linked by ribbon-development to others such in a network that, a generation hence, might spread across all England.

I went indoors. The poor old house, with its cracks and rot, would have a hard time of it to survive much more shaking of its foundations. But grief had not removed me from it, and I would obstinately resist being turfed out by the ever-increasing noise, ugliness and yobbishness: after all, my property occupied a 'slip of ground ... where a hogstye formerly stood'; and we Sussex pigs, as the old saying was, 'wunt be druv'. It could see me out. On the other hand, though I still loved it, I refused to be in thrall to it. I could imagine taking a calm and positive decision to leave for somewhere else: but only when I was good and ready to.

Audrey phoned.

'Can you come here right this minute? I have something to tell you. It won't wait.'

Oh God, I thought, as I drove down to Carlton Avenue. *Has she got herself a new bloke?*

'Look at this advert.' The local College of Higher Education was offering places to mature students on its B.A. programme. She intended to take a degree in English. She had never completed her education, having left school and home on the farm at the age of sixteen. Her excitement torrented before I had the chance to say a word. 'The moment I'd read it, I knew it was what I've got to do. That's if they accept me. I don't know whether or not I've got enough qualifications. You have to write an essay when you apply. I've not written an essay since School Cert. Do you think they'd have me? Am I too old? Have I got the brains? It'd take three years. Goodness knows what my family will think. And God only knows how I'll manage for money. I'd get a grant, though not much. But

I'm determined. Oh, but do you think I'm being daft? Do you think I ought to?'

'Whoa! Of course you must! It's a wonderful idea.'

'Oh, love, I'm so pleased you said that. I'd have gone ahead and done it in any case, mind. But I did so want your approval.'

This was the Audrey I needed, all wishy-washiness gone.

We went to Spain, entirely comfortable with each other once again. Cerros del Lago looked precisely the same as it had done a year before; but it felt utterly changed, having a different function entirely to fulfil. I showed Audrey all the places I had mentioned in my letters, and they were not as I had described. We took the ferry to Ceuta. Sitting on a locker up on deck, each of us wearing a comic straw hat, we asked a fellow passenger to take a snapshot of us. In it, we look like a parody, plumper, broadsmiling version of Ford Madox Brown's *The Last of England*.

On the journey back to England, I embarked upon a little speech. No casuistry was required for this one.

'The way I see it, about the time when you get your degree, I'll be eligible for early retirement, right?'

'Right.'

'And it's no sense, our not being together all the time, right?'

'Right.'

'So I reckon, since I can't live in your house and you won't live in mine, what we ought to do is sell 'em both and get somewhere else, right?'

'Well . . .'

'What's the problem?'

'I *could* live in your house, you know. I could *now*, you see. Maybe, if we could gradually – '

'Make it yours as well? So you won't feel you're betraying Lorna? Being an interloper, usurping her place? That what you mean?'

'Yes.'

'Listen, love. I'll tell you something I've never told you. Several times, Lorna made me promise her that if she died before me, I would find somebody else. I only agreed on condition that she'd do the same, and she did promise. It's what she wanted.'

'I know it is.'

'Oh?'

'What you've just said is one of the things she confided to me. In your kitchen, it was, one day when you were out.'

'There you are, then. Hey – wait a minute, I don't like the sound of this. What else did she confide?'

'She said there was really only one respect in which you'd ever disappointed her.'

'Oh, Lord. What was that?'

'You'd not been able to afford to give her a modern kitchen.'

'That's the first thing we'll see to. And then all the rest.'

About three weeks later, on a sunny afternoon in July, we found ourselves walking through Chichester with baritone-horn Wally and Mary, his wife. Audrey and Mary were walking a little way ahead of us men. It struck me that it might be nice to buy us all an ice-cream; but then an old near-neighbour, Ken Smith, coming from the direction of the City Cross, stopped me for a brief chat, and Wally caught up with the ladies.

'How are things going for you these days?' asked Ken, seeming to expect a mournful answer.

'Pretty good, Ken,' I said. 'And yourself and Iris?'

'Just as ever, thanks. Got your best bib and tucker on, then?'

'Yeah. Keep 'em guessing, that's what I always say. See you.'

I felt hot in my suit. When I reached the others, Mary said, 'You're a terrible man, forgetting to kiss the bride.'

She had a point. In my nervousness, and because it had been so long since the last time I'd been to my own wedding, I had forgotten that that was what one was supposed to do. It's what I did there and then. In the street, in full view. It was, and it would go on being, all right.